MAJOR POWER RELATIONS IN NORTHEAST ASIA

Win-Win or Zero-Sum Game

edited by
David M. Lampton

JCIE

Tokyo ⋏ Japan Center for International Exchange ⋏ *New York*

The surnames of the authors and other persons mentioned in this book are
positioned according to country practice.
Copyediting by Michael D. Evans and Pamela J. Noda.
Cover and typographic design by Becky Davis, EDS Inc., Editorial &
Design Services. Typesetting and production by EDS. Inc.
Printed in Japan.
ISBN 4-88907-047-8
Distributed outside Japan by Brookings Institution Press (1775 Massachusetts
Avenue, N.W., Washington, D.C. 20036-2188 U.S.A.) and Kinokuniya Company
Ltd. (5-38-1 Sakuragaoka, Setagaya-ku, Tokyo 156-8691 Japan).
Japan Center for International Exchange
9-17 Minami Azabu 4-chome, Minato-ku, Tokyo 106-0047 Japan
URL: http://www.jcie.or.jp
Japan Center for International Exchange, Inc. (JCIE/USA)
1251 Avenue of the Americas, New York, N.Y. 10020 U.S.A.

MAJOR POWER RELATIONS IN NORTHEAST ASIA

The Japan Center for International Exchange wishes to thank

The Nippon Foundation

Asia Pacific Agenda Project

Henry Luce Foundation, Inc.

Contents

Foreword

TODAY it is widely recognized that the continuing security and prosperity of the Asia Pacific region, acknowledged as the most dynamic region of the world in the twenty-first century despite the financial crisis of 1997–1999, will be largely contingent upon enhanced cooperation between the region's three dominant economies: China, Japan, and the United States. The China-Japan-U.S. Research and Dialogue Project to study the trilateral relationship was conceived by several individuals representing policy research institutions in the three countries who believed that promoting joint analysis and dialogue among them would be critical and essential in managing the future trilateral relationship. The project consists of a parent group of senior leading policy thinkers from the three countries and three study groups of emerging intellectual leaders from each country. The parent group launched the project with a workshop in Beijing in December 1996. This was followed by creation of the study group of young Japanese scholars and researchers who participated in monthly study meetings in Japan and also took part in a dialogue mission to Beijing, Hong Kong, and Shanghai in December 1996. The study group of emerging Chinese leaders participated in a dialogue mission to Tokyo in June 1997.

The first volume of essays by the three international relations experts in the parent group, titled *China-Japan-U.S.: Managing the Trilateral Relationship*, was published in 1998; the collection of essays by the group of younger Japanese intellectual leaders, titled *Challenges for China-Japan-U.S. Cooperation*, was also published that year. A volume of essays by members from both the parent senior group and the three study groups, *New Dimensions of China-Japan-U.S. Relations*, was published in 1999; *China-Japan-U.S. Relations: Meeting New*

Challenges—a second collection of essays by the three international relations experts in the parent group—was published in 2001.

This volume is the collection of papers written by young American scholars and researchers who were under the guidance of David M. Lampton and Peter F. Geithner, both China experts in the United States. The group participated in a dialogue mission to Shanghai, Beijing, and Tokyo in October 1999, where members met with Chinese scholars and representatives of research institutions and Japanese politicians and other intellectual leaders. While in Japan, the group also attended the Global ThinkNet Chiba Conference, where the first drafts of the chapters in this volume were presented.

The China-Japan-U.S. Research and Dialogue Project is a key activity under the Global ThinkNet scheme launched by the Japan Center for International Exchange (JCIE) in 1996. The Global ThinkNet—made possible by the generous support of the Nippon Foundation—is a multipronged cluster of policy research and dialogue activities designed to contribute to strengthening the Asia Pacific as well as the global intellectual policy network among research institutions and intellectual leaders.

JCIE wishes to express its sincere gratitude to the Nippon Foundation and the Henry Luce Foundation, Inc., for their financial support. JCIE is also grateful to the Asia Pacific Agenda Program for its contribution.

YAMAMOTO TADASHI
President
Japan Center for International Exchange

Introduction: Thinking Trilaterally about Big Power Relations in Asia

David M. Lampton

OUT OF HISTORICAL CONSIDERATIONS, and for expediency's sake, China appears to prefer interacting with its neighbors bilaterally. China may reason that, due to its size and potential, dealing with nations one-on-one creates a negotiating advantage. The United States seems to prefer dealing bilaterally with Asian countries as well; Washington has a legacy of bilateral security alliances in the region and is the hub of five such pacts, its participation in the ASEAN Regional Forum (ARF) and the Asia-Pacific Economic Cooperation (APEC) forum notwithstanding. However, if the central challenges confronting East Asia in the twenty-first century are to be effectively addressed, the three major powers of the region—China, Japan, and the United States—must enhance trilateral cooperation, coordination, and even joint action. The six essays in this volume concern those problems that could benefit from such trilateral cooperation and identify the major obstacles that stand in the way of such unified action.

We begin with Amy Celico's look at Chinese and American views of national security and proceed to Gregory C. May's examination of the most dangerous challenge to the three big powers' handling of Asian stability—the Taiwan issue. Next, Michael J. Green analyzes Japan-U.S. security relations, then Daniel H. Rosen examines big power economic relations in East Asia. Scott Snyder then explores South Korea's impact on big power relations, and the volume concludes with Evan A. Feigenbaum's perspective on the future challenges that societal fragmentation and political breakdown could present to China, Japan, and the United States in the years ahead—breakdowns that will require true cooperation if they are to be managed.

1999–2000: A MIXED BAG

When the initial drafts of the chapters for this volume were written for presentation at the Chiba Conference in October 1999, big power relations in East Asia were in serious turmoil along multiple dimensions. The Asian financial crisis looked as though it was winding down, but no one could be certain. Indonesia appeared to be undergoing a systemic breakdown, with international intervention in East Timor being the most obvious manifestation of the degree of the crisis. Despite the strong opposition of China and Russia, Japan and the United States were increasing their cooperation on missile defense technology research and development, partly because of an August 1998 North Korean long-range missile test over Japan. Tragically, in May 1999 a U.S. bomber mistakenly destroyed the Chinese embassy in Belgrade, Yugoslavia, during the North Atlantic Treaty Organization's (NATO) prosecution of the Kosovo War, killing three Chinese nationals and injuring more than twenty. This tragic mishap set off several days of violent anti-American demonstrations in Chinese cities and led to ongoing recriminations on both sides of the Pacific. Two months later, in July, then Taiwanese President Lee Teng-hui came dangerously close to a declaration of de jure independence when he articulated his "special state-to-state" theory in an interview with *Deutsche Welle*. This act led Beijing to immediately cancel the cross-strait dialogue, thus heightening tensions between Beijing and Taipei and fueling efforts in Taiwan and certain quarters of Washington to further tighten Taiwan-U.S. security relations. Finally, in 1999, Japan's Diet adopted, clarified, and strengthened its guidelines for Japan-U.S. security cooperation in various contingencies—a strategically worrisome move from China's perspective. Beijing assumed that the contingency Tokyo and Washington had in mind (although left unspoken) was the Taiwan Strait, rather than North Korea, which was the actual initial motivation for the move. Basically, 1999 was not a good year for cooperative trilateral relations in East Asia.

The year 2000, during which time the chapters in this volume were revised, was a comparatively more productive period in trilateral relations in East Asia. China, Japan, and the United States, along with other nations (with Australia at the helm), cooperated in stabilizing the East Timor situation, although Indonesia remained unstable. The

Asian financial crisis appeared to have ended for the region as a whole, although the need for fundamental reform in the architecture of international institutions and domestic policies that initially gave rise to the economic downturn was still obvious. Beijing and Washington effectively agreed to disagree about whether the Belgrade embassy bombing was a mistake, and in September 2000 Chinese President Jiang Zemin and outgoing U.S. President Bill Clinton had a productive meeting in New York on the fringes of the UN Millennium Summit. Of great importance, in May 2000, the U.S. House of Representatives voted by a comfortable margin to approve permanent normal trade relations (PNTR) for China as part of the bilateral agreement concerning Beijing's eventual entry into the World Trade Organization (WTO); the U.S. Senate followed suit in September, holding out the prospect that Beijing (and Taipei) would soon join the WTO. On the Korean peninsula, developments were dramatic and positive, with China encouraging North Korean leader Kim Jong Il to meet South Korean President Kim Dae Jung. A historic North-South summit of the two Korean leaders followed in the summer, along with agreements on limited family visits and indications of more restrained military behavior from Pyongyang. On Taiwan, in March 2000, the fifty-year rule of the Kuomintang Party (KMT) ended with the election of the Democratic Progressive Party candidate, Chen Shui-bian, by a plurality in a field including two other major party candidates. Although extremely unsettling to China because Chen's party charter still contained a commitment to Taiwanese independence, from his May inauguration Chen made relatively conciliatory gestures toward the mainland and at least an immediate crisis was averted. Nonetheless, the core issue of whether Taipei still adheres to even a vague "one China" concept remains the key bone of contention. This is an issue that could spark cross-strait military confrontation and thus conceivably draw in China, Japan, and the United States.

KEY CHALLENGES

Underlying these events, however, are six challenges to productive and peaceful relations among China, Japan, and the United States. It is these challenges that will provide the substance of trilateral relations in the years ahead and are also the topics of the following chapters. The challenges are not listed in any particular order and are in a number of cases interconnected. For example, Taiwan is probably the most multifaceted challenge because it is either directly or indirectly linked to every other dilemma confronting the trilateral powers—discussions of alliance relations, Sino-Japanese mistrust, and defensive technologies. Thus, we begin with the Taiwan issue.

TAIWAN

In May's contribution to this volume, we see how Taiwan is the concern that relates to practically every other issue that the trilateral countries must manage. Due to Japan's colonial past in Taiwan, the legacy of bitterness stemming from Japan's World War II invasion of China, the fact that support for Taiwan's independence is even stronger in Japan than in the United States, and because of various forms of past and present American support for Taiwan, Beijing views most issues in the trilateral relationship through the Taiwan lens. Issues of theater missile defense (TMD) focus on Taiwan, as does Beijing's mistrust of the uses to which the Japan-U.S. security alliance may be put. In short, until the Taiwan issue is stabilized, it will be difficult to deal productively and definitively with many of the other challenges in the trilateral relationship.

The core of the Taiwan problem is simple: As democracy has taken hold in Taiwan, the KMT political machine, which had as its principal identity being part of a unified China, has lost part of its raison d'être. Simultaneously, the identity of the Taiwanese people has progressively moved further away from that of China's mainland populace. Despite these developments, Beijing's determination to move toward reunification has only increased, due in part to the return of Hong Kong and Macao to Chinese sovereignty, rising Chinese nationalism, and a fear among Chinese leaders that Taiwan's drift away decreases the prospects for any type of reunification.

There are numerous reasons for the increasingly separate Taiwanese identity, but the main factors include the alienating effect of Beijing's military and diplomatic pressures on Taiwan; the natural inclination of Taiwan's emerging leaders to want to determine their own destiny rather than be submerged in a polity of 1.3 billion people on the mainland; the growing economic and social gap between the mainland and the island; past misrule of the KMT and, more recently, mounting KMT corruption; and the implied security obligations of the United States to Taiwan. The Taiwanese people ask themselves what China can offer that they do not already possess.

When Beijing looks at the situation, it has two goals—to *deter* Taiwan's independence and to *promote* an environment conducive to peaceful reunification. However, for Beijing's leaders, these goals are not equally weighted, and the means necessary to achieve one goal seem diametrically opposed to what is required to achieve the other. Of the most immediate importance to Beijing is the absolute requirement to deter Taiwan's independence, because such a development could topple not only particular leaders in China but also the regime itself. Although China's leaders would like reunification, Beijing believes that Taiwanese independence must be avoided at all costs. This, in turn, gives rise to threats to inflict military and economic damage on the island if it moves toward de jure independence. This deterrence capacity takes the form of the buildup of a short- and medium-range missile force in proximity to the Taiwan Strait. Such a buildup then inspires Taiwan's own search for a counterstrike capability, motivates Taipei to acquire TMD from the United States, and is part of the backdrop for enhanced Japan-U.S. security cooperation and Taiwan's desire to be covered under its umbrella.

If Beijing felt inclined to use military force against Taiwan, the results would be unpredictable, but assuredly negative. If the United States intervened (which is highly likely), Japan would have to decide how to actively support such an effort. Low levels of support would shatter the Japan-U.S. security alliance, in all probability setting Tokyo off on a course to achieve its future security unilaterally. This almost certainly would include increased Japanese military capabilities and the acquisition of strength that would be disquieting to many others in the region, notably China. On the other hand, if Japan joined Washington vigorously in a Taiwan conflict, this would fuel Chinese enmity that would itself power a dangerous arms competition in the region.

Furthermore, if conflict broke out in the Taiwan Strait, one could expect the transfer of antimissile technologies to Taipei and the increased likelihood of the adoption of national missile defenses in the United States and Japan. In response, this would lead to an expansion of Beijing's nuclear and conventional missile forces. Finally, the Sino-Japanese-U.S. cooperation we have seen on the Korean peninsula throughout the second half of the 1990s and into the new millennium would probably become impossible.

Therefore, handling the Taiwan issue with delicacy and foresight is the single most important item on the agenda of trilateral relations.

JAPAN-U.S. SECURITY ALLIANCE

As Green's contribution to this volume explains, the Japan-U.S. security alliance is a major concern in the trilateral relationship for a number of reasons, three of which are primary. First, as Celico recounts in the opening chapter, China is anxious about a world in which there is a sole superpower instead of multiple poles; Beijing prefers to operate in a world in which there is more room for diplomatic maneuver and balance-of-power politics. With the United States heading two alliances of particular salience to China—NATO and the Japan-U.S. security relationship—China feels surrounded. The fact that Washington talks about humanitarian and other intervention in the context of these alliances further sharpens Chinese anxieties.

Second, as Green points out, "Beijing must interpret the ambiguity over the Guidelines' [on Japan-U.S. defense cooperation in crisis] applicability to the Taiwan situation as a clear signal that unprovoked use of force in the Taiwan Strait could well be seen as a legitimate cause for Japan-U.S. defense cooperation."

Third, lurking behind all of this is the growing Japanese desire to become a "normal" country in terms of defense and security matters, and to assume what it views as its rightful place in the councils of multilateral organizations, particularly the UN Security Council. It is perhaps natural that China would hesitate to see its own power diluted by growing Japanese diplomatic and defense strength, but the legacy of past Japanese aggression against China exacerbates all of these anxieties.

This brings us to the third challenge in managing the trilateral relationship in the years ahead—the absence of genuine Sino-Japanese reconciliation after the World War II era.

SINO-JAPANESE RECONCILIATION

Just below the surface in Sino-Japanese relations lies intense Chinese resentment of Japan's past occupation of much of mainland China and the resulting mistreatment of its people. On the other hand, among Japanese there seems to be a growing belief within the current generation that it is time to stop apologizing for events that occurred long before they were born. Furthermore, there is a Japanese sense that even were Japan to definitively apologize (as it did in late 1998 to South Korea), China would never permanently forgo the short-term gains of playing on residual Japanese guilt. To an American trying to compare the China-U.S. and the Sino-Japanese relationships, it appears that in the former case the problem lies between governments, whereas in the latter case frictions appear more deeply rooted—a conflict between cultures and peoples and their respective understandings of history. This analysis suggests that, in the long run, Sino-Japanese relations will be more problematic than China-U.S. relations if the question of Taiwan can ever be put behind China and the United States.

The requirements for what needs to be done to improve Sino-Japanese relations are clear; the ability to carry them out, however, is in doubt. Japan needs to unambiguously renounce its imperial past in Asia, whereas China must be willing to accept that renunciation and move forward, leaving the guilt card unplayed. Without the requisite trust that such reconciliation would build, neither country's inevitably greater international and security role will be reassuring to the other, and the resulting distrust would become one more layer making big power cooperation in the region improbable. Such cooperation is essential not only to manage the Taiwan issue but also to underpin the cooperative economic policies necessary for sustained and stable economic growth throughout the region and to address the problem of security and stability on the Korean peninsula and in the region more broadly (as Feigenbaum discusses in his chapter).

These are the challenges to which we now turn and that will receive further attention in the chapters to follow.

INCREASING DEFENSE TECHNOLOGIES

During the cold war, because the Soviet Union and the United States had enormous offensive strategic nuclear strike capabilities and the ability to defend against such weapons was nearly nonexistent, the two superpowers agreed that there was no realistic (affordable and reliable) alternative to the doctrine of mutual assured destruction (MAD). Thus, in the 1972 Anti-Ballistic Missile (ABM) Treaty, the two superpowers agreed to largely forgo the development and deployment of such defensive systems. Moscow and Washington decided not to pursue these systems for the simple reason that, were they developed and deployed on a large scale, they would only provide incentives for each side to dramatically increase its respective number of offensive weapons, thereby overwhelming any likely defensive system's capabilities—each side would end up with less security, at a greater cost. Furthermore, defensive systems put a hair trigger on each side's strategic nuclear arsenal because each national command authority would fear that if it did not launch its missiles before an initial strike hit, then the few missiles remaining in its inventory after the strike would be neutralized by the opponent's defense, leaving the victim naked without an effective retaliatory capability. In short, the American public was willing to accept MAD because there was no realistic alternative.

Recent and possible near-term technological developments, when combined with the collapse of the Soviet Union (which has dramatically reduced the size of the arsenal with which a hypothetical defense must cope) and the potential rise of small nuclear states with long-range strike capability, have reopened the debate over defensive systems. Popularly elected politicians find it hard to forgo systems that offer even the remote possibility of protection from obliteration. In today's America, there is substantial momentum behind a possible future decision to deploy defensive systems (for defense of the U.S. homeland and America's friends and troops stationed abroad). If the development and deployment of national and TMD systems occur, the impact on trilateral relations will be substantial, somewhat un-predictable, and probably destabilizing.

Although a great deal would depend on the negotiations surrounding possible deployment of defensive systems and on who has such possible systems, the likely underlying dynamic is clear. Beijing will respond by increasing the survivability of its strategic systems and their number; indeed, China already is moving in these directions, and the U.S. deployment of defensive systems would probably just intensify these efforts. This, in turn, will increase anxiety levels in Japan and elsewhere in Asia (including India). These nations will re-act in a number of ways, including developing their own defensive and deterrent systems that, in turn, will further energize the Chinese buildup. In the end, everyone in the region will forgo opportunities for economic growth and cooperation and the region will be more insecure.

The Taiwan issue simply adds more escalatory potential to this dynamic. If Beijing continues to gradually increase its short- and medium-range missile force opposite Taiwan, the pressure on the is-land to develop its own deterrent of some sort, and the desire to ob-tain some defense, will be strong. Indeed, Taiwan President Chen has already stated as much. In such a setting, Taiwan's requests for defensive technologies will become more persuasive in Washington. Furthermore, this same Chinese buildup will also increase anxieties in Japan. The likely responses from Tokyo and Washington would further inflame the tensions with Beijing over Taiwan and heighten China's mistrust of the Japan-U.S. security alliance.

In short, if defensive technologies prove feasible and affordable, they will present a grave challenge to the management of the China-Japan-U.S. relationship. The way out of the worst aspects of this di-lemma is to resolve some of the underlying concerns and to negotiate some combination of offensive and defensive weapons restraints, when and if defensive systems become a realistic possibility.

TRILATERAL ECONOMIC COOPERATION

There are many reasons why it is exceedingly difficult for the three nations to pursue mutually reinforcing economic policies, not the least of which is that economic performance is inextricably linked to domestic politics and considerations of domestic power. Basically, domestic politicians do what they perceive as necessary for domestic politics, and the requirements of the international economic system generally take a back seat.

Beyond this basic point, however, Rosen notes another important consideration: "The longer-term basis of the trilateral relationship requires substantial regime building to help nurture and maintain economic growth, and this is a task made difficult by the present tendency for political and security friction to delay proactive cooperation to strengthen regimes." The Asian financial crisis points to the need for the three powers to rethink their individual domestic economic policies and their respective policies toward crisis cooperation and, more broadly, to reassess what changes may be necessary in international/multilateral economic institutions. There is little evidence that the three countries have moved far in this direction.

Such delay is dangerous beyond the ever-present volatility that massive and instantaneous capital flows present to global and regional economic stability. The United States has had nearly a decade of uninterrupted economic expansion, and China has had an even longer period of rapid economic growth. During this period of expansion, the United States has been the export market of last resort for ailing Asian economies, as well as for China's dynamic export machine. Because it is difficult to believe that the laws of the business cycle have been entirely nullified, some day there will likely be a setback in the American expansion. When unemployment begins to rise, American receptivity to massive levels of imports may be severely tested, thereby generating conflict with China and Japan, as well as other exporting Asian countries.

The United States is not the only country for which an economic downturn could make it a more difficult economic partner. China's ability to cooperate on exchange rate stability from 1997 to 2000 was facilitated by continuing positive, albeit slowing, economic growth. If the Chinese and American economies are simultaneously beset with deteriorating growth (not to mention ongoing Japanese economic problems), the management of trilateral economic relations (e.g., exchange rates, trade deficits, market access, capital flows) is going to be much more difficult. The time to put in place cooperative economic policies and institutions is during a growth phase, not a contraction phase. In this sense, the impending entry of Beijing into the WTO is a hopeful sign.

THE KOREAN PENINSULA

A brief discussion of the Korean peninsula comes last, not because it is viewed as the least important problem, but rather because it illustrates the importance of cooperation between the trilateral countries in effectively addressing the problems enumerated above. As Snyder points out in his chapter, "The situation on the Korean peninsula affects and is affected by the triangular China-Japan-U.S. relationship as well as the nature and the quality of the respective bilateral relationships." Without the cooperation of Beijing, Tokyo, and Washington, along with far-sighted policy in Seoul, it is far from clear that stability could have been maintained on the Korean peninsula over the second half of the 1990s and into the new century. The costs of breakdown would have been (and remain) incalculable.

In the Korean dilemma, we see clearly the best rationale for Sino-Japanese-American cooperation. When these three powers are harnessed together to deal with problems, the outcome is at a minimum acceptable to all three players, and to the region more broadly. However, if they work at cross-purposes, or are in conflict, managing even second-order problems becomes much more difficult. In short, conflictual relations among China, Japan, and the United States are costly in their own terms, in addition to rendering the region and the world far less capable of dealing with their many other problems. To facilitate cooperation, leaders in Beijing, Tokyo, and Washington must work together on the agenda of issues discussed above and detailed in the pages that follow.

MAJOR POWER RELATIONS IN NORTHEAST ASIA

1 🌿 Chinese and American Views of National Security

Amy P. Celico

We learned in Kosovo, as in Bosnia and Rwanda, that in this era of varied and mobile dangers, gross violations of human rights are everyone's business. In recent weeks, we confronted not only Milosevic, but ethnic cleansing. NATO's leaders simply refused to stand by and watch while an entire ethnic community was expelled from its home in the Alliance's front yard. By acting with unity and resolve, NATO reaffirmed its standing as an effective defender of stability and freedom in the region . . . And it underlined the importance of the leading nations on both sides of the Atlantic acting together in defense of shared interests and values.
—*Secretary of State Madeleine Albright, June 28, 1999*

Human rights will always fall within a country's national jurisdiction as long as our planet is divided into countries and people live in those countries. The human rights problems in any country, big or small, powerful or weak, have to be settled by that country's own government in full independence and by reference to the people. That is a fundamental principle. The Chinese government and people oppose any interference in a country's domestic affairs in the name of a "humanitarian crisis."
—*President Jiang Zemin, October 25, 1999*

I N THE IMMEDIATE AFTERMATH of the North Atlantic Treaty Organization (NATO) intervention in Kosovo, the China-U.S. relationship was once again badly strained, exemplifying only one area of disagreement to bedevil the bilateral relationship at the end of the

The views expressed in this chapter are those of the author and do not necessarily reflect the official policy or position of the U.S. Department of State or the U.S. government.

twentieth century. Even if the central issue of Taiwan is taken out of the equation, tensions between China and the United States have risen over a number of events since the autumn of 1998, including the passage of revised Guidelines for U.S.-Japan Defense Cooperation legislation in the Japanese Diet, Japan-U.S. joint research on theater missile defense (TMD), American discussions about deployment of national missile defense (NMD), domestic American allegations over Chinese spying activity, and the May 1999 accidental bombing of the Chinese embassy in Belgrade. The relationship has suffered as a result of these tensions and, despite the predominant shared areas of interest, the relationship has entered the new millennium in a precarious state.

This chapter seeks to analyze the undercurrent fostering recent tensions and the growth of differences between the two countries that have emerged with the end of the cold war. China and the United States place differing degrees of importance on the universal concepts of sovereignty and equality—an unsurprising difference given the disparate ideologies that define the two countries and their relative standing in the world today. This translates into a fundamental obstacle to good China-U.S. relations; the United States seeks to maintain its present global primacy, whereas China seeks to right the imbalance of a unipolar world. Not exactly a collision course—partially because China is not presently in a position to alter the status quo and partially due to overriding shared interests—but not a recipe for harmony either.

In the evolving post–cold war international environment, China and the United States have laid out their strategies for meeting new and traditional threats in public documents on national security. The United States has characterized its national defense strategy as one that promotes an American leadership role in the world to meet its goals of ensuring the continued security, prosperity, and freedom of the American people. In October 1998, the White House published the *U.S. National Security Strategy for a New Century*, highlighting the maintenance of U.S. forward-deployed troops and the strengthening of existing security alliances as the two bedrock principles of the American defense strategy. One month after this document was published, the U.S. Defense Department released its latest iteration of the *United States' Security Strategy for the East Asia Pacific Region*, better known as the *East Asia Strategy Report* (EASR), which outlined how this global defense strategy would be implemented in the region. As this third post–cold war EASR reflects, the United States continues to view its sustained engagement in East Asia in the twenty-first century as essential to address security threats and maintain regional stability in an area of the world that allows the United States to conduct approximately $500 billion a year in transpacific trade (U.S. Department of Defense 1998, 6–7).

In its first broad-based national defense white paper, published in the summer of 1998,[1] China acknowledged that it also seeks to "lead a peaceful, stable, prosperous world into the new century" (Office of the State Council of the People's Republic of China 1998, 4–5). This white paper, like the EASR that followed it four months later, focused not only on national defense policy but also on the changed international security environment driving this policy. Like Washington, Beijing sees conflicts, along with transnational security threats, as the new leading sources of global instability. To respond to these threats, China has added to its traditional strategic focus of security for survival the additional task of maintaining economic security as a basis for its defense strategy. For China watchers, one of the most interesting parts of this document was China's explanation of its New Security Concept. China posited this new concept as a way to safeguard peace and placed it in stark contrast to the "cold war mentality" of relying on bilateral alliances.

Taking into consideration these latest explanations of national defense policy, the question remains: How different are Chinese and American views of national security? This chapter discusses the two aforementioned key tenets of the 1998 *China Defense White Paper*—the global security environment and China's national defense strategy. The white paper highlights the security goals that China and the United States share in terms of increased military transparency, responsibility for economic and political stability, a desire to enhance security cooperation and dialogue, and the willingness to work to maintain a peaceful international environment. On comparing the white paper with American national security policy, it is obvious that the two countries have similar broad national security interests. As many nations in the region have pointed out, a good China-U.S. relationship, where both sides focus on their common interests and goals, is necessary for a stable, peaceful Asia Pacific in the new millennium. And this relationship is possible only when China and the United States focus on these common national security interests and goals rather than allow their differences to drive the relationship.

Unfortunately, since the end of the cold war era, the idea that shared interests between the two states will foster good relations has been challenged. In the post–cold war era, American policymakers have placed new emphasis on economic security and humanitarian intervention, two tenets of international security that were outside the realm of traditional cold war strategic thinking. Chinese leaders share American interests in the former but vehemently oppose adoption of the latter. Economic security is easy to embrace in the post–cold war world where nations share the benefits of increased trade and finance cooperation. But humanitarian intervention, a "practice in search of a theory," in Elliott Abrams' (2000, 73) words, erodes the foundations on which the Chinese continue to build their foreign policy and relies much on the continued American primacy that China is seeking to diminish.

In recent discussions on security issues, it is clear that academics and policymakers in China have been profoundly affected by the NATO intervention in Kosovo (particularly the May 1999 bombing of the Chinese embassy in Belgrade), and the 1998 white paper does not fully reflect this latest strain of thinking in Chinese security circles. U.S.-led NATO actions have altered the way Chinese view the international security environment as well as China's role in this brave new world. Indeed, in officially sanctioned works, China has started to question its perception that the post–cold war era has resulted in an enhanced rather than a diminished security environment, and the United States is increasingly being viewed as the chief contributor to China's sense of insecurity. This shift, whether temporary or permanent, is a feature of the present, post-Kosovo era, and has clear implications for China and the United States, as well as other Asia Pacific countries.

A sense of hedging permeates the Chinese and American viewpoints of the global security environment and their respective national defense policies, in turn fueling mistrust and the perceived need to shore up for the possibility of future competition. This chapter does not seek to prescribe solutions to the current dilemma. Instead, by taking a deep look at the post–cold war security environment and the development of China's national defense policy, it attempts to root out the similarities and differences in Chinese and American national security outlooks. The goal of this overview is to provide a better understanding of why a good bilateral relationship will continue to be difficult, but by no means untenable, in the twenty-first century.

THE POST–COLD WAR
INTERNATIONAL SECURITY ENVIRONMENT

In the post–cold war security environment, China and the United States face no direct threat of military invasion, and this change has brought about a general relaxation in the international security environment. However, this environment and its ensuing path toward globalization is dynamic and uncertain. A host of transnational threats challenge both countries: the proliferation of weapons of mass destruction (WMD), drug trafficking, terrorism, financial instability, resource depletion, environmental degradation, and uncontrolled refugee migration. Although they differ on some prescriptions for dealing with these threats, Beijing and Washington recognize that maintaining economic security has become a shared challenge in an era of globalization and interdependence.

In response, both countries have adopted the promotion of economic prosperity as a key tenet of their national security strategies. President Bill Clinton has argued that the United States has profound interests at stake in the health of the global economy, and he saw American economic and security interests as being inextricably linked (The White House 1998, iv, 27). Likewise, in his political report to the Fifteenth Communist Party Congress in September 1997, President Jiang Zemin cited globalization in support of his call for deepening domestic economic reform and privatization of state-owned enterprises (*People's Daily* 22 September 1997, 2, overseas edition). In international affairs, too, China contends that economic security plays an increasingly important role in its "comprehensive concept of security" and maintains that different nations' cooperation in the economic sphere should form the basis for global and regional security.

China has highlighted the dangers of ignoring economic security by likening the losses suffered during the recent Asian financial crisis to a regional war. To achieve a comprehensive recovery of the Asian economy, China called on the countries of the region to enhance financial cooperation, as it pledged to do its part to promote domestic economic growth and stability, and to work with its neighbors to rebuild the regional economy the same way. The United States viewed the Asian financial crisis as "a core security concern" and was committed to playing a leading role in mitigating the national and international effects of the setbacks the region has suffered (U.S. Department of Defense 1998, 67).

To combat these common threats in the present international environment, China and the United States have advocated enhancing multilateral security cooperation and strengthening international institutions. As China sees it, these multilateral forums offer important channels for governmental and nongovernmental dialogue that will lead to increased mutual understanding and confidence between countries. In the same way, international institutions provide avenues for the settlement of divergences and disputes among nations through peaceful means. The United States also seeks strengthened international institutions as a means to ensure its security and has stated that international cooperation is vital because many of the threats the world faces cannot be adequately addressed by any single nation.

Although the two countries agree on the need for multilateral cooperation, they differ over the structure of such cooperation. This divergence springs from the way in which they view the global security environment. China wants the post–cold war international environment to form the foundation for a truly multipolar world. For the Chinese, in this environment, cooperation would be based on the precepts of sovereignty and equality. The United States, however, still sees its leadership role as vital for the maintenance of cooperative security and has increasingly begun to challenge the traditional inviolability of state sovereignty. Washington continues to rely on its strength to shape the global security environment.

Since the post–cold war era began, China has voiced its distrust of this American presumption. After former President George Bush declared a New World Order in 1991, however vague the actual concept, the United States was accused of taking advantage of its unique status as the sole remaining superpower to establish an international order based on American values and favorable to its own interests (Pan 1991). In response to the Bush declaration, China posited its time-tested Five Principles of Peaceful Coexistence (first enunciated at the Bandung Conference in 1955) as the foundation for a new international political order. These principles are mutual respect for territorial integrity and sovereignty, mutual nonaggression, mutual noninterference in internal affairs, equality and mutual benefit, and peaceful coexistence.

In standing by the Five Principles as the bedrock of its foreign policy, China, like the United States, has pledged to continue to regard safeguarding peace as an obligation of its national defense. But, as one Chinese analyst enunciated, sovereignty is the fundamental interest that determines a nation's survival and development (Fang 1994). In defining its own national security policies, China has criticized America's "new interventionism" as an infringement on other countries' sovereignty and therefore their national interests. This is at odds with the American perception of its national security policy —that its leadership role has a positive, active, and stabilizing influence on the international security environment.

This contradiction simmered throughout the 1990s. Simultaneously, China has become increasingly dissatisfied with the development of the post–cold war international security environment. First, the Chinese watched as the Clinton administration followed its predecessor's declaration of a New World Order with a strategy for maintaining America's global predominance. In this role, according to the 1997 *Quadrennial Defense Review*, the essence of the American defense strategy is threefold: to *shape* the international security environment in ways favorable to U.S. interests, to *respond* to the full spectrum of crises when directed, and to *prepare* now to meet the challenges of an uncertain future (U.S. Department of Defense 1997).

Furthermore, the Chinese have witnessed what they consider to be American attempts to reorient the norms that have long governed the behavior of states. Wilsonian ideals are now challenging the traditional concept of respect for state sovereignty, most recently exemplified in the Kosovo intervention. China was shocked to see U.S.-led NATO circumvent the United Nations in deciding to intervene in Kosovo and worries that such a precedent could similarly challenge Chinese actions some day or have implications for such issues as Tibet,

Taiwan, and Xinjiang—issues Beijing considers its internal affairs.

How has the United States justified its "shaping behavior"? Mainly with the argument that the post–cold war world is a place where collective security must include a common moral component. The United States is the world's only remaining superpower and, as such, has little incentive to act in ways antithetical to its own national interests. Because American national security policy revolves around the strategy of maintaining alliances and a global forward military presence to deter potential rivals, American efforts to expand multilateralism have been limited, mainly relying on bandwagoning behavior by allies to achieve America-defined objectives. Nations around the world have been largely willing to bandwagon in the recognition that the benefits of an alliance with America outweigh the risks of diplomatically going it alone (e.g., see Bell 1999).

For Beijing, this kind of American leadership strikes a cautionary note and reinforces suspicions that American actions around the globe have direct implications for China. Although the tenets that define American global leadership in this new century continue to be subject to debate, even those opposed to the present Clinton administration's course of action hold views that alarm China. On one hand are those who argue that today's relatively benevolent international environment is the product of American hegemonic (read: moral and democratic) influence and must be maintained through increased defense spending and NMD, lest other nations be allowed to play a larger part in shaping the world to suit their needs (see Kagan and Kristol 2000, 61). Others argue that American hegemony could be used to foster greater international cooperation. For example, Richard Haass (1999, 43), in an essay entitled "What to Do with American Primacy," argues that multilateralism, while limiting, is the best way to foster a world that protects U.S. interests. Furthermore, Haass insists that a post–cold war international society be built on four pillars —one being a limited doctrine of humanitarian intervention based on the recognition that people, not just states, enjoy rights.

For all of China's progress toward integration into an international system, it is a system founded in the Peace of Westphalia that interests China, one that recognizes the sovereignty of nations as inalienable. In the words of Deng Xiaoping (1993, 331, 347–348), "National sovereignty and national security should be the top priority; national rights (*guo quan*) are more important than human rights," and the latter should by no means be allowed to undermine the former.

How has Beijing reacted and adjusted its national security policy to American views and behavior? With a new awareness that its own national interests could be sacrificed to American goals, China's security strategy shifted in the 1990s. As a result, China has sought to play a more involved role in international affairs, especially in regional matters, partially to offset American influence. China is increasingly critical of America's role in the new international security environment and is actively pursuing greater multilateralism to combat what it views as Washington's cold war behavior. This shift was first publicly enunciated in China's New Security Concept, a platform unveiled in 1997 and codified in the 1998 *China Defense White Paper*. The United States—and China's neighbors—continues to monitor China's more proactive national security strategy. The United States wants to reassure the Chinese leadership that U.S. actions are not aimed against China and, in turn, it is hoped the evolution of Chinese strategy will not include altering the status quo in East Asia.

China's National Security Strategy

COLD WAR SECURITY STRATEGY

In the Chinese context, military doctrine, which is determined at the highest levels of political and military leadership, provides the political vision of the nature of war and the military guidance for the armed forces to follow (Huang 1994, 11). In Maoist China, the doctrine for the People's Liberation Army (PLA) was the "people's war," which relied on the political nature of revolutionary warfare and took advantage of China's huge landmass and the mobilization of its population to "lure the enemy troops in deep so as to crush them one by one." By the mid-1980s, Chinese political and military leaders had reached a consensus that China was facing a relatively peaceful international environment and that total war was unlikely. Under Deng Xiaoping's modernization program, Mao Zedong's total war doctrine was adjusted and became the "people's war under modern conditions." Codified as a "strategic transformation" by the Party Central Military Commission in 1985, the leadership began to focus on the type of armed conflict that China might encounter under new "modern conditions"—specifically high-density, high-tech conflict, or "local war."

Although China intensified its military modernization, Deng's first priority was economic reform and development. Aside from territorial disputes, there appeared little indication that China had any inclination to modernize its military for reasons other than improved self-defense. In international affairs, Deng shifted China's traditional approach in drawing its foreign policy lines according to the social system and ideology of a country to an emphasis on dealing with international relations based on national interests.[2] Furthermore, China's principal threat, the Soviet Union, was in the process of downsizing its military presence in East Asia by the late 1980s, and China took advantage of this reduced threat to proceed with a policy of improving its peripheral relationships in the region.

POST–COLD WAR NATIONAL SECURITY STRATEGY

With the advent of the post–cold war era, China acknowledged a general relaxation in the international security environment. Chinese security analysts assumed that American power would gradually diminish as a bipolar world was replaced by a multipolar one, as policymakers continued to adjust China's security strategy to focus on protecting economic development, and as America was debilitated by internal problems. Beijing's national security strategy emphasizes the necessity of preventing war from breaking out while simultaneously ensuring that any conflict be kept outside China's territory. Military planners, shocked by the high-tech superiority the United States demonstrated in the Gulf War (and subsequently Kosovo), advocated that China should undertake its own "revolution in military affairs." As a result, national security strategy also called for the continuation of China's active defense modernization program. As Chinese analyst Yan Xuetong concluded in a 1995 discussion of China's security strategy, "while China's security environment has been improved, it has not yet solved all problems related to the defense of its security. Therefore the fundamental aim of China's security strategy remains the enhancement of its security defense" (1995, 3–4).

Even though this enhancement was meant primarily to safeguard economic security as well as to mitigate the widening gulf between China's military capabilities and those of the United States, some of China's neighbors reacted cautiously to China's defense modernization program—with its strategic focus on defending China's periphery and, thus, steadily increasing defense spending. Beijing's strategic objective for its defense modernization goals remains (as it has been since the 1950s) to build armed forces capable of defending China against any external threat and to permit Beijing to pursue its foreign policies without the restrictions created by limited military capabilities (Godwin 1996, 486–487). Yet, with China enhancing its military and engaging in provocative actions in the South China Sea, fears of a nascent "China threat" had begun to spread by the mid-1990s (e.g., see Eikenberry 1995 and Lee 1997).

To counter the "China threat" argument and to meet the needs of its defense strategy in the new international security environment, China began to support enhanced bilateral and multilateral security cooperation. In its bilateral relationships, China has highlighted the principle of "not directing (relations) against a third country," a tenet of collective security that China maintains marked the cold war era. In support of the trend toward multipolarization, Chi Haotian, China's defense minister, enunciated the theme of "desiring peace, seeking cooperation and promoting development . . . [through] the use of dialogue and consultations to resolve security issues" ("Chi Haotian on Military Diplomacy" 1998, 7). China reversed its long-held opposition to and isolation from East Asian regional institutions. Concrete examples of Chinese engagement in multilateralism in the 1990s included China's participation in the ASEAN Regional Forum (ARF), support for international law, the release of its 1995 white paper on arms control, and the joint development schemes it has put forward for handling overlapping claims to islands in the South China Sea.

China's 1998 white paper contributed to an enhanced understanding of the nature of China's defense modernization and its security strategy. The white paper more closely tied China into the global community of responsible actors through its continued emphases on arms control and disarmament, the defensive nature of China's defense policy, the civilian leadership of the PLA, and an increased level of transparency in its discussion of China's defense budget composition. Two additional emphases are the promotion of China's New

Security Concept and its national defense strategy toward the Asia Pacific region.

CHINA'S STRATEGY TOWARD ASIA PACIFIC

As David Finkelstein (1999, 8) has noted, China's New Security Concept is as much about what China is "against" as what China is "for." The New Security Concept has three parts, all outgrowths of China's vision of the post–cold war security environment. These parts include conducting relations based on the Five Principles of Peaceful Coexistence, strengthening mutually beneficial economic cooperation, and promoting mutual understanding and trust through dialogue and cooperation to peacefully resolve disputes among nations (Office of the State Council of the People's Republic of China 1998). Dissatisfied with the slow progress toward multipolarization, the New Security Concept was promulgated to offer an alternative to the post–cold war unipolar world—a truly multipolar international community that would cooperate in economic and security realms for the mutual benefit of all its members.

Chinese participation in the Asia-Pacific Economic Cooperation (APEC) forum and ARF are examples of China's increased willingness in the post–cold war era to use regional multilateralism to promote its interests in East Asia.[3] Indeed, the 1999 track-one meeting in Beijing for ARF foreign affairs and defense officials, "A Professional Program on China's Security Policy," hosted by the Foreign Affairs College of China, gave China an opportunity to showcase its increased transparency and sell its New Security Concept to members of the security forum. The New Security Concept was promulgated, in part, to present China's defense policies in a more reassuring light to its East Asian neighbors. As China has discovered, regional recognition of its new economic power allows it to play a positive and more dominant role in such forums. Also, in its relationship with the Association of Southeast Nations (ASEAN), China has found a sympathetic ear to its precept of noninterference in the domestic affairs of other countries and a common opposition to Western standards of human rights. In Northeast Asia, China accepted trilateral economic talks among itself, Japan, and South Korea; Beijing has also worked closely with the United States to encourage North and South Korea to continue the Four-Party Talks and convene the historic 2000 North-South Summit.

In its bilateral relationships, too, China maintains that its partnerships with the big powers of Asia Pacific constitute an important contribution to regional security because these relationships are not "directed against a third country." Concurring with this view, Robert Ross (1997, 34) highlights China's efforts to consolidate regional trends and promote stability as a striking development in its foreign policy. He uses as examples policies toward Russia, North and South Korea, Thailand, Myanmar, and the countries of Indochina, Central Asia, and South Asia to show that China has emphasized cooperative measures to consolidate existing relationships rather than forceful measures to promote new patterns of relations.

In the late 1990s, China had considerable success in making the improvement of bilateral relations with nations on its periphery a leading foreign policy objective to augment its national security— the case of India notwithstanding. However, China's steps toward increased multilateralism, while welcome and important, may be frustrated if its desired rules governing multilateral behavior are not shared, especially outside East Asia. The New Security Concept was offered for the international community of nations at large—not just East Asia. The NATO intervention in Kosovo, the first real test of China's New Security Concept since its enunciation the preceding year, highlighted the fundamental, systematic differences between China and the United States that could hinder cooperative multilateral action in the future.

THE KOSOVO EFFECT ON
CHINESE NATIONAL DEFENSE POLICY

Well before Slobodan Milosevic began his campaign against ethnic Albanians in Kosovo, in the West there had been sympathy for humanitarian intervention in the defense of democratic values. In Leslie Gelb's words, "failure to do something about mass murder and genocide corrodes the essence of a democratic society" (1994, 6). For NATO, the atrocities committed against ethnic Albanian Kosovars compelled a response to halt the violence. Indeed, German Chancellor Gerhard Schroeder likened the mass killings in Kosovo to Nazi genocide in eliciting sympathy for NATO's cause. But for the Chinese government, overriding the principle of sovereignty is unjustifiable. The 1998 white paper, in setting the rules for participation in UN peacekeeping operations, maintained that "military means should not be resorted to even for humanitarian ends" (Office of the State Council of the People's Republic of China 1998, 17).

When NATO intervened in Kosovo without the approval of the United Nations, China pointed to its white paper's concern over the dangers posed by "hegemonism and power politics." The Kosovo intervention confirmed for China that the United States was more powerful than ever and that the current international security environment possessed insufficient means to bridle American predominance. NATO's actions also raised questions in China concerning the bounds of this "new interventionism," and whether China's initial assessment that the post–cold war security environment was more stable had been too optimistic.

In addition, in the Kosovo case, China became concerned that the NATO bombing of Yugoslavia set a number of precedents. Its first concern was that foreign intervention has become acceptable not only to alleviate humanitarian suffering but also to forcefully resolve ethnic conflicts of the kind that China faces in Tibet and Xinjiang. Second, China worried that a strengthened NATO will now be the model for security cooperation in the Asia Pacific region, based on the Japan-U.S. alliance and American forward-deployed troops. And the third concern is that American unipolarity will remain a defining characteristic of the twenty-first century security landscape.

In the immediate aftermath of the Kosovo intervention (and simultaneously with the U.S. debate over TMD and NMD), military strategists called for increased defense spending to counter further American action that could be directed against China. The Chinese government allowed its media to publish caustic tirades against American hegemony for the remainder of 1999, in no small part fueled by the mistaken bombing of the Chinese embassy in Belgrade. In a sense, the public, with official acquiescence, was venting against perceived American injustice not only with regard to the embassy bombing and NATO intervention but also against American support for Taiwan, U.S. complaints about China's human rights record, the May passage of enhanced Defense Guidelines in the Japanese Diet, and American discussion of TMD and NMD deployment. Chinese concerns of encirclement were on the rise.

Unspoken have been China's moves to offset the precedents Kosovo has set. In the post-Kosovo era, there remains a question of whether the events in southeastern Europe will bring long-term harm to the China-U.S. relationship. Over the past decade, China and the United States have continually engaged in hedging behavior, lest one country truly turn antagonistic toward the other. Certainly the Kosovo intervention, and China's reaction to it, will reinforce this hedging. Started well before NATO's intervention in Kosovo, China has been seeking to chip away at American predominance by improving bilateral relationships with its neighbors—American friends and foes alike—to mitigate against its fears of containment.

However, in its own public assessments of the NATO intervention published at the end of 1999, China's leadership concluded that the "megatrend" of the times has not changed—the international situation is moving toward relaxation, and schemes to establish a unipolar world will fail. Chinese Foreign Minister Tang Jiaxuan (2000) recently wrote that, although destabilizing factors and uncertainties in international politics had significantly increased, and the journey toward multipolarization would be a "lengthy and tortuous process," in this volatile international situation, big countries must continue to compromise and cooperate to meet their mutual interests. And so, aside from rhetoric, China has not done anything fundamentally aimed at a realignment of the global or regional security environment. It can be argued that China is at too early a stage of development to shoot the moon and challenge the United States, and that China is biding its time until the country has enough military power and domestic stability for such a move. The "China threat" argument rests on such a view.

Yet, although the Chinese leadership is dissatisfied, it is fully cognizant that maintaining peace is its primary national interest. And this interest is shared with the United States. This is not threatening behavior; it is rational. Beijing and Washington act in a hedging manner with the realistic view that they may well be competitors in the twenty-first century. In the meantime, both recognize that cooperation furthers both of their individual national security policies. We can expect many more rhetorical disagreements between China and the United States in the coming years. The relationship will continue to be rocky. But the confrontations will be limited for as long as both countries see their stable bilateral relationship as a necessity to maintain international peace, thereby allowing the United States to maintain its predominance and China to consolidate its position as a powerful country.

China posits that a multipolar world is the way of the future; the United States does not. Both support multilateral forums in East Asia and, most recently, the UN-sanctioned, humanitarian operation in East Timor. But China continues to charge that the unipolar, "cold war mentality" of the United States, as reflected in the NATO intervention in Kosovo and the U.S. policy of strengthening its alliances in East Asia, is out of step with this trend toward a truly multipolar world. Herein lies another deep cleavage in a shared China-U.S. view of national security policy. The United States asserts that American leadership is precisely the venue for prolonged international peace in the post–cold war era. According to U.S. strategic logic, as this system and its alliances mature, countries opposing world peace will recognize that they pose no credible threat to this stable status quo and will be deterred by the prospect of sure defeat. Of course, as Kim Jong Il, Saddam Hussein, and Usama bin Laden so readily have demonstrated, the U.S.-led system has not cowed the world into subservience. Overriding individual cases, like Kosovo, these men represent the post–cold war threats to national security that China and America share, including the proliferation of WMD, opaque military spending, and terrorism. Because these threats are shared, China and the United States continue to work toward an understanding of how to best protect their shared national security interests through increased cooperation, even while they reserve the right to differ in specific policy actions.

CONCLUSION

Although there are abundant examples of differences between the Chinese and American views of national security, there also exist overriding similarities between the two vantage points. Developments in Chinese post–cold war strategic thinking, most recently outlined in the 1998 *China Defense White Paper,* which highlighted the need for mutual security, enhanced transparency, and support for confidence-building measures and multilateral institutions, reflect the American vision for a stable, peaceful international environment in the twenty-first century. China and the United States have shared visions of the importance of maintaining economic security to sustain domestic growth. Although China can remain critical of the American "excessive reliance" on military power to achieve security, China too has highlighted the fundamental importance of developing its national defense. And although China refutes the preoccupation with bilateral alliances, China emphasizes its own web of strategic partnerships recently forged with the Central Asian republics, Russia, Japan, South Korea, the United States itself, and the European Union to guard against any one threat.

Although the two nations share some similarities, this chapter has attempted to highlight the developments since the end of the cold war that have deepened the existing cleavage between Chinese and American national security policies. The remaining fundamental differences, which will be difficult to overcome in the near term, are related to the concepts of sovereignty and equality. In the international security environment, China and the United States both underscore the need to work together to overcome transnational security threats and peacefully resolve local wars. However, the two sides differ where China feels its own security is threatened. For the Chinese leadership, examples of these threats include passage in the Japanese Diet of the enhanced Guidelines for U.S.-Japan Defense Cooperation, the American strengthening of its global alliance network, NATO's intervention in Kosovo, and U.S. discussion of NMD and TMD deployment. China sees these developments as threatening to its own national security interests and territorial integrity. Although Washington may worry that Chinese actions could increase instability in the region, China fears American actions will impinge directly on its sovereignty.

Although the 1998 *China Defense White Paper* has not adequately clarified when and how China will act to resolve security threats (should peaceful means fail), the paper was an important step toward the kind of transparency that will make misperceptions easier to overcome. The United States should similarly work to increase the transparency behind its policy decision-making process to allay Chinese fears and possible misperceptions. Just as China is striving to develop a strategy for preserving its national security, so is the United States. Domestic American debates about the wisdom and practicality of humanitarian intervention and NMD/TMD deployments are examples of this development. The United States should make clear, and China should above all recognize, that foreign policy decision making in a democracy can be a messy undertaking. Invariably, different constituencies will try to involve themselves in the process and the result.

Shared interests will drive American and Chinese policies, but diverging values and perceptions will continue to inhibit cooperation. This is a sober but realistic assessment. Without a common enemy, as the two countries shared during the latter stages of the cold war, it will be more difficult to find areas of cooperation, but that makes the quest no less important. The only answer for this incarnation of the classic security dilemma is to increase trust, and the first step toward this goal is to continue security dialogue. On a bilateral basis, efforts to this end temporarily stalled in the wake of the accidental bombing of the Chinese embassy in Belgrade. Restarting this dialogue was difficult, as domestic considerations in both countries seemingly hijacked this important work. But resumption of this dialogue was eventually achieved in recognition of overriding shared national interests. China's neighbors have consistently told Beijing and Washington that they rely on good China-U.S. relations to maintain regional harmony.

Continued multilateral dialogue among the United States, its allies, and China is another essential needed to replace suspicion with trust, and defensive posturing with true cooperation, and thus further mutual security in the post–cold war world. The United States should continue to maintain a high level of transparency in its regional bilateral alliances and increase multilateral initiatives in the region. In the same way, Washington should recognize that its actions contribute to China's sense of insecurity. Regardless of the legitimacy of Chinese perceptions, the United States should take actions to reassure Beijing. China, too, must act in ways that consistently reassure its neighbors that it is a status quo power, with no ambition to drive out or replace American leadership in the Asia Pacific region.

Stronger China-Japan-U.S. trilateral relations should be the focus of this multilateralism in East Asia. As the Japan-U.S. alliance continues to be strengthened so too should trilateral relations be deepened to ensure regional stability and allay Chinese concern about the Japan-U.S. security alliance. Although ARF will never replace either the Japan-U.S. alliance or any other bilateral American relationship in the region, it can be one effective multilateral channel for increased understanding and cooperation. Effective trilateral relations could be another channel. In both arenas, the United States must work on having China come to terms with the long-term American vision of remaining in Asia Pacific.

American and Chinese global concepts of national security are not so different—both sides see the same transnational threats and both advocate greater multilateralism, economic security, improved bilateral relations, and the maintenance of robust national defense capabilities. Developments since the end of the cold war have brought about new areas of disagreement and have accentuated the differences that remain. If their national security strategies could be amended to include policies that enhance mutual security as well as their individual national interests, the remaining gaps between China and the United States, which will dominate twenty-first century security thinking, could begin to be substantively addressed.

NOTES

1. China's first white paper on arms control and disarmament was published in 1995.

2. Yong Deng (1998) cites the Chinese authors Peng Guangqian and Yao Youzhi for this statement.

3. Yuan Jing-dong (2000) has dubbed recent Chinese behavior "conditional multilateralism," characterized by a low degree of institutionalization. The author argues that this behavior reflects China's ambivalence toward its place in Asia Pacific and its interactions with other major players in the region.

BIBLIOGRAPHY

Abrams, Elliott. 2000. "To Fight the Good Fight." *The National Interest* 59(Spring): 70–77.

Albright, Madeleine. 1999. "After Kosovo: Building a Lasting Peace." Remarks delivered at the Council on Foreign Relations, New York. 28 June.

Bell, Coral. 1999. "American Ascendancy and the Pretense of Concert." *The National Interest* 57(Fall): 55–63.

"Chi Haotian on Military Diplomacy." 1998. *Beijing Review* (30 January): 7.

Deng Xiaoping. 1993. *Deng Xiaoping wenxuan* (The selected works of Deng Xiaoping) (Vol. 3). Beijing: Renmin chubanshe.

Eikenberry, Karl W. 1995. "Does China Threaten Asia-Pacific Regional Stability?" *Parameters* (Spring): 82–103.

Fang Ning, Colonel. 1994. "Defense Policy in the New Era." *China Military Science* (Winter). Cited in Michael Pillsbury, ed. 1997. *Chinese Views of Future Warfare*. Washington, D.C.: National Defense University Press.

Finkelstein, David. 1999. "China's New Security Concept: Reading between the Lines." *Washington Journal of Modern China* 5(1): 6–13.

Gelb, Leslie H. 1994. "Quelling the Teacup Wars." *Foreign Affairs* 73(6): 2–6.

Godwin, Paul H. B. 1996. "From Continent to Periphery: PLA Doctrine, Strategy and Capabilities Towards 2000." *China Quarterly*, no. 146: 464–487.

Haass, Richard N. 1999. "What to Do with American Primacy." *Foreign Affairs* 78(5): 37–49.

Huang, Alexander Chieh-ching. 1994. "Chinese Navy's Offshore Active Defense Strategy: Conceptualization and Implications." *Naval War College Review* (Summer): 7–32.

Jiang Zemin. 1999. Interview with the newspaper *Le Figaro*, Paris. 25 October.

Kagan, Robert, and William Kristol. 2000. "The Present Danger." *The National Interest* 58(Spring): 57–69.

Lee Tai To. 1997. "East Asian Assessments of China's Security Policy." *International Affairs* 73(2): 251–262.

Office of the State Council of the People's Republic of China. 1998. *China Defense White Paper*. Beijing: Office of the State Council of the People's Republic of China.

Pan Tongwen. 1991. "Gai yao fen xi bu shi de xin shijie ge" (A preliminary analysis of Bush's new world order). *Guoji wenti yanjiu* (International studies) 42(October): 15–19, 26.

Ross, Robert S. 1997. "Beijing as a Conservative Power." *Foreign Affairs* 76(2): 33–44.

Tang Jiaxuan. 2000. "Opportunities Overweigh Challenges, Hopes Outnumber Difficulties." Ministry of Foreign Affairs: The People's Republic of China. <http://www3.itu.int/missions/China/tjxuan.htm> (14 January 2000).

U.S. Department of Defense. 1997. *Quadrennial Defense Review*. Washington, D.C.: U.S. Department of Defense.

———. 1998. *1998 East Asia Strategy Report*. Washington, D.C.: U.S. Department of Defense.

White House, The. 1998. *U.S. National Security Strategy for a New Century*. Washington, D.C.: The White House.

Yan Xuetong. 1995. "Lengzhan hou zhongguo de dui wai anquan zhanlie" (China's post–cold war security strategy). *Contemporary International Relations* 5(5): 23–28.

Yong Deng. 1998. "Conception of National Interests: Realpolitik, Liberal Dilemma, and the Possibility of Change." In Yong Deng and Fei-ling Wang, eds. *In the Eyes of the Dragon: China Views the World.* New York: Rowman & Littlefield Publishers, Inc.

Yuan Jing-dong. 2000. *Asia Security: China's Conditional Multilateralism and Great Power Entente.* Carlisle, Penn.: Strategic Studies Institute, U.S. Army War College.

II ⚓ Taiwan's Role in the China-Japan-U.S. Trilateral Relationship

Gregory C. May

THE CONTINUED SEPARATION of Taiwan from mainland China is a major obstacle to better relations between China, Japan, and the United States. Like other difficulties in the trilateral relationship, the Taiwan issue is deeply rooted in history. Japan's colonization of Taiwan from 1895 to 1945 was one of many indignities China suffered at the hands of imperialist powers during its "century of humiliation." The United States' protection of and aid to Taiwan—Chiang Kai-shek's last base after his defeat on the mainland in 1949—prevented the unification of all of China under the Chinese Communist Party (CCP).

Today, the CCP regime continues to blame Japan and the United States for perpetuating cross-strait political division, which is now in its sixth decade. The United States continues to maintain a steady supply of weapons to the island, and Beijing complains loudly that Tokyo and Washington, through their newly strengthened security alliance and proposed development of a theater missile defense (TMD) system, are providing Taiwan with military cover to pursue a permanent break from the mainland. Furthermore, in the eyes of Chinese leaders, Japan and the United States are expanding their political contacts with Taiwanese authorities in direct violation of their respective normalization agreements with China.

With the possible exception of the Korean peninsula, the Taiwan Strait is the region where China, Japan, and the United States are most likely to become involved in a military conflict. The cross-strait missile tensions in the spring of 1996 gave the world a hint of how such a confrontation could develop and expand to include Japan and the United States. In March 1996, as the Taiwanese prepared to vote in the island's first-ever direct presidential election, the People's

Liberation Army (PLA) "test-fired" ballistic missiles into water just outside of Taiwan's major ports, with at least one of the missiles flying over northern Taiwan (Gellman 1998). This display of force was meant to deter Taiwan from seeking independence. In response, the United States dispatched two aircraft carrier battle groups to the area in the greatest display of American force in East Asia since the Vietnam War. One of the carriers (ironically, the *Independence*) was based in Yokosuka, Japan.

The ability of China and Taiwan to resolve their differences peacefully will be a deciding factor in whether the China-Japan-U.S. relationship will evolve toward greater cooperation or continue to be rife with tension and latent hostility. Although cross-strait negotiations will be the primary means for reaching a solution to the Taiwan issue, the actions of Japan and the United States will be critical both for ensuring the survival of the status quo and for fostering an atmosphere conducive to a peaceful resolution. This chapter discusses two major trends in the Taiwan Strait that will require careful management by Beijing, Tokyo, and Washington (and, of course, Taipei) to avoid a repeat of March 1996, or worse. The first trend is the growing dissatisfaction in China and Taiwan with the status quo, which, although filled with ambiguity and half-truths, has nevertheless succeeded in maintaining peace and stability for most of the last half century. The second trend, closely related to the first, is the issue of the remilitarization of Taiwan, which is occurring even as cross-strait economic contact continues to flourish. Finally, the chapter offers some recommendations for how China, Japan, the United States, and Taiwan can work together to shore up the status quo so that it can survive until such a time as Beijing and Taipei are able to create a new framework for their relationship.

THE FRAGILE STATUS QUO

The status quo in Taiwan has undergone a severe beating in recent years. Until 1999, one could define the status quo as the continued separation of mainland China and Taiwan under the "one China" principle (though both sides defined "one China" differently) with both Taipei and Beijing committed to eventual reunification. In July

1999, however, Taiwanese President Lee Teng-hui announced that relations between the two sides should be conducted on a "special state-to-state" basis. By suddenly abandoning the idea of a single Chinese state (even though the concept was far from reality), Lee damaged the "one China" consensus that had helped keep the peace between China and Taiwan for most of the last half century. Lee's successor, Chen Shui-bian—a pro-independence, yet pragmatic, politician—has promised not to incorporate the "state-to-state" formula into Taiwan's constitution but, at the time of this writing, he had yet to concede to Beijing's demand that Taiwan reembrace the "one China" principle. To the extent Taiwan still adheres to "one China" at all, it is to the idea of "one China" as a cultural and ethnic, but not political, entity. With Taiwan's commitment to "one China" weakening, China is growing less comfortable with the idea of a continued separation across the Taiwan Strait and, as indicated in Beijing's February 2000 Taiwan policy white paper, has threatened to use force if Taiwan delays reunification talks indefinitely. The status quo has not completely collapsed—Taiwan remains nominally committed to eventual reunification and President Chen has promised not to abolish Taiwan's Guidelines for National Reunification—but it is in need of repair and reinforcement if it is to survive long enough for a peaceful settlement to be reached.

TAIWAN IN THE POSTNATIONALIST ERA

Taiwan has undergone tremendous political change in the past two decades. These changes fall into two broad categories. The first transition, Taiwan's evolution from an authoritarian one-party regime into a multiparty democracy, has been well documented and has won wide praise in the international community. But the second transition, involving the decline of Chinese nationalist ideology and the emergence of a Taiwan-focused national identity, is not as well understood or appreciated by outside observers (including those in China).

Arguably, it is the second evolution that has had the greatest impact on cross-strait relations. Although the lifting of martial law in 1987 is often cited as the turning point for Taiwan's political reforms, an equally important watershed occurred in 1991. On May 1 of that year, President Lee declared an end to the "Period of Mobilization for Suppression of the Communist Rebellion," thus officially calling a halt to the Chinese civil war. As part of this process, the ruling Kuomintang Party (KMT) renounced its pledge to retake mainland China by force (a threat that was never very credible) and passed constitutional changes to make the two parliamentary bodies, the National Assembly and the Legislative Yuan, democratically elected from constituencies in Taiwan and the smaller Taiwan-controlled islands of Penghu, Kinmen (Quemoy), and Matsu. Soon thereafter, the aging lawmakers who were elected on the mainland in 1947—and continued to serve after the 1949 retreat of the Republic of China (ROC) government to Taiwan—were retired. More than any other event, this change signaled the KMT regime's transition from an exiled Chinese government to a government of Taiwan.

These reforms sparked an intense, often rowdy, debate over the nature of Taiwan's relationship with mainland China. On one end of the spectrum were "old-guard" Chinese nationalist stalwarts—typically mainlanders who arrived in Taiwan with Chiang Kai-shek—who resisted the Taiwanization of the KMT under Lee, himself a native Taiwanese who felt more comfortable speaking Japanese than Mandarin. At the opposite end of the spectrum were the Taiwanese nationalists—many of whom had been persecuted during the martial law era and formed Taiwan's first opposition group, the Democratic Progressive Party (DPP)—who pushed for a formal declaration of Taiwan's independence from China and the establishment of a new Taiwanese republic. Vice President Hsiu-lien Annette Lu is emblematic of this strongly pro-independence group.

Since Lee's election as Taiwan's first democratically elected president in March 1996, this polarization of Taiwanese politics has decreased and a new mainstream "Taiwan consensus" has emerged that stresses Taiwan's status as a country politically independent from China, but still part of a broadly defined Chinese civilization. A core aspect of this consensus is the idea that ROC/Taiwan (the terms are now used interchangeably by Taiwanese leaders) is already an independent, sovereign state, and therefore a declaration of independence is unnecessary. This concept was first articulated by then DPP Chairman Shih Ming-teh in 1995 and later adopted by Lee and the KMT. Hence, the debate in Taiwan is no longer simply over reunification versus independence. Rather, Taiwanese political groups are engaged in a more nuanced deliberation over the best way to maintain Taiwan's de facto independence from Beijing while simultaneously consolidating the island's impressive economic and political accomplishments.

The new "Taiwan consensus" also emphasizes harmony between Mandarin-speaking mainland Chinese, who make up roughly 15 percent of Taiwan's population, and the native Taiwanese majority, whose ancestors arrived in Taiwan from China as far back as 400 years ago. The passage of time and intermarriage are rapidly blurring this mainlander-Taiwanese distinction. In the 1998 parliamentary and mayoral election campaign, Lee coined the slogan "new Taiwan person" to emphasize that all groups on the island, regardless of when they or their ancestors arrived on Taiwan, are Taiwanese.

The polling data shown in figure 1 illustrate the emergence of this new Taiwan-based identity. The number of Taiwan residents who identify themselves exclusively as "Chinese" fell steadily from almost 50 percent in 1993 to just above 13 percent in April 2000. At the same time, the number identifying themselves only as "Taiwanese" increased from under 20 percent to 42 percent over the same period. Meanwhile, a relatively steady number on Taiwan, just under 40 percent, continue to describe themselves as "Taiwanese and Chinese." For now at least, a majority on Taiwan still appear to acknowledge at

Figure 1: Self-identification of Taiwan Residents

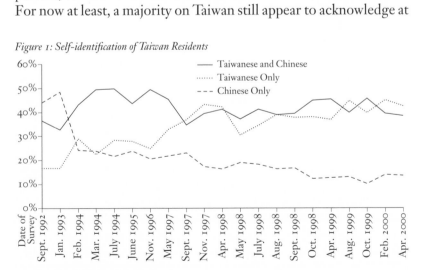

SOURCE: Mainland Affairs Council (2000).

least an ethnic and cultural link to China. This connection, however, does not mean support for reunification. Public opinion polls show more than 70 percent of the people on Taiwan reject Beijing's vision of reunification under a "one country, two systems" formula, even given that China has offered more generous terms to Taiwan than what it granted to Hong Kong and Macao (Mainland Affairs Council 2000).

The strength of this "Taiwan consensus" and the growing maturity of Taiwan's democracy were demonstrated in the March 2000 presidential election. The three major candidates—the KMT's Lien Chan, KMT breakaway James Soong Chu-yu, and the DPP's Chen Shui-bian—advocated largely identical proposals for cross-strait relations that emphasized Taiwan's sovereignty and independence from China coupled with offers to begin political talks with Beijing on the basis of equality. Chen emerged victorious in a tight three-way race with 39 percent of the popular vote (Lien and Soong split the potential KMT vote, winning 23 percent and 37 percent, respectively), but only after moving to the center by distancing himself from his past advocacy of formal independence—that is, a "Republic of Taiwan"—and the pro-independence platform of his own party. With a "Taiwan first" political philosophy and defiance of Beijing's contention that Taiwan is merely a Chinese province, Chen is viewed by many in Taiwan as the inheritor of Lee's political legacy.

At the beginning of the twenty-first century, Taiwan has a love-hate relationship with the status quo. On one hand, the status quo has allowed Taiwan to realize the many gains outlined above while still remaining outside of Beijing's control. On the other hand, Taiwan's leaders have thoroughly rejected China's definition of the "one China" principle because they feel China has unfairly used "one China" to constrict Taiwan's international breathing space and force Taipei into the subordinate role of a local government. Taiwan is also concerned that its ambiguous status leaves it open to pressure from the United States to enter into reunification talks with China. In a March 24, 1999, speech, U.S. Assistant Secretary of State for East Asian and Pacific Affairs Stanley Roth suggested that "interim agreements" between Taipei and Beijing might be helpful for improving cross-strait relations. Taipei interpreted these remarks (wrongly, according to the Clinton administration) as being part of a larger

U.S. effort to pressure Taiwan to enter into political negotiations on Beijing's terms (Mann 1999b).

As it attempts to clearly establish its sovereignty, Taipei has consistently chipped away at the "one China" pillar of the status quo. During the martial law years, the KMT maintained that there was only one legitimate government of China—the ROC government temporarily located in Taipei—and that the mainland was a rebel-controlled area. In 1992, Taiwan adopted a "one country, two political entities" policy that held that Taipei and Beijing were rival, but equal, administrations within a single Chinese state.[1] Finally, on July 9, 1999, Lee announced in an interview that Taiwan and China should deal with one another on a "special state-to-state" basis, somewhat analogous to the relationship between the former East and West Germany (Government Information Office 1999). In his May 20, 2000, inaugural address, Chen attempted to diffuse the cross-strait tensions by promising that so long as China does not use force against Taiwan, his government would not declare independence, change Taiwan's official name from the "Republic of China," incorporate the "state-to-state" formula into Taiwan's constitution, hold a referendum on independence, or abolish the Guidelines for National Reunification and the National Unification Council—the so-called five no's (Chen 2000). Chen's administration, however, has not explicitly repudiated the "state-to-state" formula, but has merely pledged not to mention the phrase that offends Beijing. Chen himself remains ambiguous on reunification, though he has spoken of the possibility of forming a confederation with China. "Only the 23 million residents of Taiwan have the right to decide which way they will go in the future," Chen said at his first press conference in June 2000 (Office of the President 2000). Although Chen, like his predecessor, holds open the possibility of a future "one China" (Mainland Affairs Council 1999b), Taiwan has nevertheless departed, perhaps irreversibly, from its strongly pro-reunification stance of the 1970s and 1980s.

REUNIFICATION IS RISING ON CHINA'S AGENDA

A steady decline in pro-reunification sentiment on Taiwan; the DPP's rise to power; the impression of expanding security ties between Taipei, Tokyo, and Washington; and the domestic political need in China to maintain the momentum of Hong Kong and Macao's return are all causing the Taiwan issue to rise on Beijing's agenda. Whereas Mao Zedong spoke of reunification taking one hundred years, Chinese officials are now stressing the need to make faster progress. In a speech marking Macao's return to Chinese sovereignty on December 20, 1999, Chinese President Jiang Zemin said that "we have both the determination and the ability to resolve the Taiwan question at an early date" (Jiang 1999). Two months later, on February 21, China's State Council issued a white paper on Taiwan policy that, in addition to repeating previous threats to use force if Taiwan declared independence or was occupied by a foreign power, threatened military action if "the Taiwan authorities refuse, *sine die*, the peaceful settlement of cross-strait reunification through negotiations" (Information Office of the State Council 2000, 4–5). The increasing sense of urgency on the mainland is heightening anxieties in Taiwan, where officials are reluctant to enter into political talks without first establishing Taiwan's equality (and Lee's "special state-to-state" remark was part of this effort). In this atmosphere, any attempt by China to set a clearly defined schedule or deadline for reunification would be destabilizing.

Because of its ideological constraints, however, China has been unable to take proactive measures to stop the "independence drift" it sees on Taiwan. It is impossible for Chinese leaders to admit, at least publicly, that reunification may not be the genuine desire of the Taiwanese people and that an overwhelming majority of the Taiwanese want to remain separate from the motherland for the foreseeable future. Rather than address fundamental issues, such as the large political and economic gap across the Taiwan Strait, Beijing preferred to scapegoat Lee as an individual, just as it blamed the Dalai Lama for its difficulties in Tibet. The aftermath of Lee's "special state-to-state" comment saw a new nadir in cross-strait discourse with the *People's Daily* accusing Lee of "treason" and of being a "criminal to the nation" (Unsigned editorial 1999). In the months following Lee's retirement, the mainland press refrained from harsh criticism of Chen, though it viciously attacked Vice President Lu, whom the *People's Liberation Army Daily* labeled the "scum of the nation" (Cheng 2000). Chinese leaders appear oblivious to the fact that such attacks on Taiwan's elected politicians only create ill will among the

Taiwanese public and reinforce the CCP regime's general disdain for democracy.

China also faces additional ideological constraints in the form of Deng Xiaoping's legacy. Deng originally articulated "one country, two systems" as a flexible model for reunification with Taiwan. Unfortunately for Beijing, the application of this formula to Hong Kong has caused it to lose any appeal it may have had for the Taiwanese, who now firmly associate "one country, two systems" with Hong Kong's subordination to Beijing and the roll-back of democracy and civil liberties in the former colony. But again, China has difficulty changing tactics because "one country, two systems" is part of the Deng canon that is a key source of legitimacy for the present leadership.

As a result of the dramatic changes in Taiwan and China's inability to respond to them, the overriding trend of cross-strait relations in the 1990s was the disconnect between the political relationship, which had gotten worse, and the economic relationship, which continued to play a mitigating role in an otherwise tense situation. By 1998, Taiwan's cumulative investment in mainland China had reached $40.4 billion (Mainland Affairs Council 1999a, 24) and, according to an estimate by Tung Chen-yuan (1999, 231), Taiwan-funded enterprises in China may have accounted for as much as 20 percent of China's total exports in 1996. But economics alone is not enough to ensure continued stability. Although China holds out the prospect of more economic cooperation as a carrot to Taiwan, the truth is that Taiwan already enjoys most of the benefits of China's vast consumer market and cheap labor pool, even in the absence of direct trade. For example, Taiwanese companies control nearly half of China's market for instant noodles (Moore 1999, 28), and Taiwanese electronics companies have already shifted 29 percent of their computer component manufacturing to the mainland (Baum 1999). Business interests on both sides, however, have had limited influence over policy. Beijing largely ignored the sentiments of leaders in Fujian and Guangdong provinces who were concerned about losing Taiwanese investment when it embarked on its missile exercises of 1995 and 1996 (Lam 1999, 178–179). Similarly, Lee successfully resisted pressure from foreign and Taiwanese business leaders to lift restrictions on direct cross-strait trade (though Chen has vowed to reevaluate these policies).[2] The fact that the political relationship across the Taiwan Strait grew more tense in the 1990s, even as cross-strait trade boomed, demonstrates that economic contact alone cannot be a substitute for effective dialogue and a stable political relationship.

JAPANESE AND U.S. REENGAGEMENT WITH TAIWAN

As China and Taiwan grow increasingly dissatisfied with the present situation, Japan and the United States are emerging as the primary defenders of the status quo. Despite its ambiguities, the status quo has served the interests of Tokyo and Washington well by allowing both countries to conduct normal political and economic relations with China, while still enjoying fruitful "unofficial" ties to Taiwan. Because a military crisis over Taiwan would be so potentially damaging to East Asian security—not to mention the strains it would cause in the Japan-U.S. alliance—Japanese and American officials tend to emphasize stability in the Taiwan Strait as an end in itself. Although China and Taiwan share this desire for peace and stability, they also have competing interests. As seen in 1995 and 1996, Beijing is willing to raise tensions to discourage Taiwan from moving toward independence. Taipei, as witnessed in Lee's "special state-to-state" comment, is also willing to risk instability to assert its claim of equality vis-à-vis China.

Like China, the United States is struggling to adjust to the dramatic changes that have taken place on Taiwan. Breaking diplomatic relations with Taipei and canceling the ROC-U.S. Mutual Defense Treaty was the price Washington had to pay for normalizing relations with Beijing in 1979. This disengagement from Taiwan, though controversial in the United States, was made easier by the fact that the KMT government was at the time a harsh authoritarian regime with a spotty human rights record and, like Beijing, it clung to a "one China" formula that precluded dual recognition. Also, the opportunity to cooperate with China to oppose the Soviet Union provided a compelling strategic rationale to justify casting Taiwan aside.

Both of these factors changed in the 1990s. The collapse of the Soviet Union and the end of the cold war weakened the strategic underpinnings of the China-U.S. relationship. In addition, the Tiananmen Square violence of 1989 heightened U.S. criticism of China's human rights record and caused many Americans to draw comparisons between the repression in mainland China and the political liberalization taking place on Taiwan. Although Washington's "one China" policy—meaning continued recognition of China as the sole legitimate government of China—never came under serious attack, growing sympathy in the United States for Taiwan led to a partial reengagement with Taipei in the 1990s.

Militarily, the 1979 Taiwan Relations Act, which commits the United States to provide Taiwan with defensive weapons, has gained ground over the August 1982 Sino-American Joint Communiqué, in which Washington pledged to gradually scale back such sales. Throughout the 1990s, the United States increased arms sales to Taiwan in qualitative and quantitative terms. Most significant was the 1992 decision to sell 150 F-16 fighters to Taipei. Between 1989 and 1998, the United States agreed to provide Taiwan with the Patriot antimissile system, seven Perry-class frigates, five Knox-class frigates, 300 surplus M-60A3 tanks, and 74 Avenger surface-to-air missiles, among other equipment (International Institute for Strategic Studies 1999, 178–179). In the spring of 2000, the United States was seriously deliberating the sale of four Aegis destroyers to Taiwan and eventually delayed a decision pending a Department of Defense study on Taiwan's defense needs. In addition to weapons sales, Taiwan and the United States have expanded their strategic dialogue since the March 1996 crisis and have increased the number of private, high-level contacts between military and civilian leaders (Mann 1999c). For example, in October 1998, Taiwan's then chief of the General Staff, Tang Fei, met in Washington with U.S. Defense Secretary William Cohen and Chairman of the Joint Chiefs of Staff Henry Shelton. Meanwhile, many members of the U.S. Congress have advocated scrapping the U.S. policy of strategic ambiguity—which implies U.S. intervention in the Taiwan Strait may not be forthcoming if Taipei provokes a crisis—with one containing explicit and unconditional guarantees to defend Taiwan.

Politically, Washington has also significantly upgraded its unofficial relations with Taiwan. In 1992, the Bush administration allowed U.S. Trade Representative Carla Hills to travel to Taipei, the first cabinet-level official to visit Taiwan since 1979. Later, as part of its 1994 Taiwan policy review, the Clinton administration endorsed the idea of allowing regular cabinet-level contact with Taiwan to discuss economic and technological matters. Since the review, four cabinet-level U.S. officials have visited Taiwan: Transportation Secretary Federico Peña in 1994, U.S. Small Business Administration head Philip Lader in 1996, Energy Secretary Bill Richardson in 1998, and Transportation Secretary Rodney Slater in 2000. These developments, coupled with Lee's high-profile 1995 trip to Cornell University, led China to conclude that Washington was in practice restoring government-to-government ties with Taipei even though Washington continued to characterize such contact as "unofficial."

The U.S. government as a whole continues to have difficulty finding the proper balance between maintaining a "one China" policy, which is necessary for upholding the status quo, and promoting unofficial relations with Taiwan. In May 1995, under intense pressure from Congress, the Clinton administration infuriated China by granting Lee a visa to visit Cornell University, where Lee received his Ph.D. in 1968. In June 1998, President Bill Clinton attempted to compensate by explicitly stating U.S. opposition to Taiwan independence, "two Chinas," or Taiwan's inclusion in organizations in which statehood is a requirement for membership—the so-called three no's (White House Office of the Press Secretary 1998). Critics of the "three no's" statement say President Clinton deviated from past U.S. policy, which simply emphasized the need for a peaceful solution without elaborating what that solution should be (e.g., see Yates 1998). Fearful that Washington was pressuring it to accept mainland China's terms for a political settlement, Taipei reacted bitterly to the "three no's" and began a policy review that eventually led President Lee to announce his "special state-to-state" model ("Re-definition of China Ties" 1999).

Japan, too, has also partially reengaged a democratic Taiwan, but not nearly to the same extent as the United States. Since China and Japan normalized ties in 1972, Taiwan has been a secondary issue in China-Japan bilateral relations. Overall, Japan has scrupulously observed the "one China" principle and unofficial ties between Japan and Taiwan have been kept at a much lower level than Taiwan-U.S. relations. A November 1991 meeting between Taiwan's Economics Minister Vincent Hsiao Wan-chang and Japan's Minister of International Trade and Industry Watanabe Kōzō, which occurred during an Asia-Pacific Economic Cooperation (APEC) forum conference in

Seoul, was the first cabinet-level contact between Tokyo and Taipei since 1972. A similar cabinet-level meeting took place at the October 1994 APEC meeting in Osaka, but such talks are still rare.

Unlike the United States, Japan has given little support for Taiwan's "pragmatic diplomacy" campaign. In 1994, the Japanese government pressured the Olympic Council of Asia to rescind its invitation to Lee to attend the opening ceremonies of the 12th Asian Games in Hiroshima. Likewise, Japanese authorities refused to allow Lee to attend the 1995 APEC leaders summit in Osaka or to make a Cornell-style visit to Kyoto University, where Lee studied during World War II.

Taiwanese officials have openly criticized Japan's deference to mainland China. In his 1999 book *Taiwan de zhuzhang* (Taiwan's viewpoint), Lee writes, "It is regrettable that Japan is the weakest in standing up to mainland China . . . on all matters Japan asks for instructions from Communist China. This is true on matters of history as well as policy" (240–241). One reason for this frustration is the limited ability of pro-Taiwan constituencies in Japan to influence policy. As in the United States, Taiwan enjoys strong support among Japan's elected representatives. For example, a group of 177 Diet members from the Liberal Democratic Party lobbied in 1995 to have Lee invited for an unofficial visit ("Japanese MPs" 1995). Also, local politicians, such as Tokyo Governor Ishihara Shintarō, have expressed support for upgrading relations with Taiwan ("Tokyo Governor's Pro-Tibet" 1999). (In November 1999, Ishihara became the highest-ranking Japanese official to visit Taiwan since 1972.) However, Japan's highly centralized foreign policy apparatus, which concentrates power in the hands of the Foreign Ministry, leaves pro-Taiwan groups in Japan with much less leverage than their American counterparts enjoy.

Japan would like for Taiwan to remain a second-tier issue in its relations with China. The security threat posed by North Korea is a higher priority for Japan, and Tokyo wants to secure Beijing's cooperation in dealing with the erratic Pyongyang regime. But, even as it strictly adheres to a "one China" policy, Japan is finding it more difficult to steer clear of the cross-strait dispute. The strengthening of the Japan-U.S. alliance, which allows Tokyo to play a more prominent role in supporting American forces, and Japan's participation in the U.S. TMD system, which Beijing fears will be extended to Taiwan, are elevating cross-strait issues on the China-Japan bilateral agenda.

Beijing also sees signs that Japan is no longer as willing to accommodate China on the Taiwan question. Japanese leaders have indicated Taiwan lies within the scope of the Japan-U.S. alliance[3] despite Chinese demands that Taiwan be explicitly excluded. Also, during Jiang Zemin's November 1998 visit to Tokyo, the late Prime Minister Obuchi Keizō refused to issue his own "three no's" pledge on Taiwan. In an August 1999 interview, the Chinese ambassador to Japan, Chen Jian, expressed a common sentiment among China's leadership when he said, "The main external obstacles to China's reunification process come from two countries, namely, the United States and Japan. There is indeed a force in Japan which is sympathetic toward, supports, and encourages Taiwan independence" (Chang 1999).

DANGER OF AN ARMS RACE IN AND AROUND THE TAIWAN STRAIT

The weakening of the status quo outlined above is contributing to a second worrisome trend in the Taiwan Strait: a nascent, but accelerating, arms race. In its urgency to make progress toward reunification, Beijing has scrapped its conciliatory policy of the early to mid 1990s —exemplified by Jiang's "eight point" speech of January 1995[4]—in favor of a more hard-line approach that stresses military intimidation. This new strategy came into full play after Lee's visit to Cornell University when the PLA test-fired missiles into waters near Taiwan in July 1995 and again in March 1996. When cross-strait tensions were raised again by Lee's "special state-to-state" announcement of July 1999, China responded with military threats, including intrusions by mainland fighters into Taiwanese airspace and the staging of amphibious landing exercises. Although China's leaders continue to express a desire for a peaceful solution and refer to Jiang's eight points, such statements are made against a backdrop of increasingly prominent military pressure. China's buildup of short-range ballistic missiles on its side of the Taiwan Strait and its refusal to renounce the use of force indicate that the military "stick" will remain a key part of China's Taiwan policy.

Modernization of the PLA is thus essential if China is to maintain a credible military deterrence against Taiwanese independence. No longer tasked with fending off a massive Soviet land invasion, the PLA is now focusing on gaining the ability to protect Chinese interests in littoral areas, especially the Taiwan Strait. The PLA's efforts to reduce the size of its large land army (currently estimated to number more than 1.8 million personnel) (International Institute for Strategic Studies 1999), acquire modern fighter aircraft and ships, expand its arsenal of short-range ballistic missiles, and develop "power projection" technologies, such as in-flight refueling, are all consistent with this goal.

Although the PLA does not pose a direct threat to American military preponderance, the PLA's capacity to inflict damage on U.S. forces is increasing. For example, the PLA recently acquired Russian "Sunburn" missiles that were designed by the Soviets for attacks on American aircraft carriers. China's military modernization also poses serious policy dilemmas for Washington, which has committed itself to help Taiwan maintain adequate defenses. If the United States continues to increase the quantity and quality of weapons sales to Taiwan in response to the PLA's advances—possibly fulfilling Taiwan's request for new submarines and missile defense technology—then China-U.S. relations will suffer. But the alternative, restricting sales to Taiwan and allowing the military balance to tilt progressively toward China, is also dangerous. If it felt U.S. security commitments were weakening, Taiwan could revive the nuclear weapons program it was pursuing as recently as 1988 (Albright and Gay 1998) and, perhaps more likely, develop offensive delivery vehicles. In a July 1995 speech, President Lee made reference to Taiwan's abandoned nuclear program and remarked that the question of whether Taiwan needs its own nuclear weapons would "require long-term study" ("Taiwan Has No Plans" 1995). In December 1999, then Vice President Lien Chan said Taiwan should acquire long-range, surface-to-surface missiles to "develop a reliable deterrent force, and strengthen our second-strike capability." (Lien, however, did not mention what kind of warheads such missiles would carry [Bodeen 1999].) A cross-strait missile and nuclear weapons race would represent a worst-case scenario in terms of regional stability, not to mention U.S. anti-proliferation efforts.

The problems of maintaining stability and discouraging an arms race are compounded by the changing nature of warfare. Even when the battles themselves take place in a limited geographic area, modern conflicts increasingly require a global array of assets. Satellites are important for guiding precision weapons, locating and tracking targets, and gathering intelligence. New concepts about information warfare and the use of computer viruses and other electronic weapons to damage an enemy's computer networks raise the prospect of the Internet becoming a secondary battlefield. (China and Taiwan engaged in a "cyber war" of sorts in the summer of 1999 when computer hackers on both sides of the Taiwan Strait succeeded in altering the government websites of the other [Wang 1999]). New military innovations could mean that the United States will no longer be able to guarantee Taiwan's defense simply by selling guns, planes, and ships to the island without also providing Taiwan better access to America's military information infrastructure.

Taiwan's possible participation in a future upper-tier TMD system (capable of intercepting missiles in space) raises some fundamental questions about information sharing and Taiwan's relationship to the Japan-U.S. alliance. Because upper-tier TMD will likely rely on American space-based sensors, China fears that inclusion of Taiwan in a future missile defense system would involve "hard wiring" the island into a regionwide network providing real-time missile launch and tracking data. The fact that Beijing sees TMD as a Japan-U.S. "joint venture"—Tokyo pledged in August 1999 to split up to $524 million in TMD research and development costs with Washington (Sims 1999)—makes the idea all the more intolerable to China. With an estimated 200 short-range missiles deployed opposite Taiwan, and 50 more added every year (Blair 2000), China could probably overwhelm any TMD system covering Taiwan (TMD is not expected to be able to counter massive strikes of more than a few dozen missiles). However, whether TMD can effectively protect Taiwan is less important to Beijing than the linkages such a system would create between Taiwan, Japan, and the United States—connections Beijing says would make Taiwan a de facto member of the Japan-U.S. alliance. China's officials have indicated that Beijing would respond to missile defense by deploying even more advanced ballistic missiles.[5]

STRATEGIES FOR MANAGING THE TAIWAN ISSUE

The ambiguous relationship between Taiwan and the Japan-U.S. alliance ensures that Taiwan will continue to be a major irritant in the trilateral China-Japan-U.S. relationship for the foreseeable future. China's fear of a possible U.S. intervention in the Taiwan Strait, with Japan in a supporting role, is eclipsing the benefits Beijing once saw in the alliance as a check on Japanese remilitarization. Resolution of the Taiwan question in a manner satisfactory to Beijing and Taipei would remove a significant barrier to greater China-Japan-U.S. cooperation. But given how far away reunification seems at present, all sides will need to give careful attention to the Taiwan issue to avoid a new crisis. Even in the absence of any kind of official trilateral dialogue, there are several strategies China, Japan, and the United States can adopt to better manage the Taiwan issue. These include the following.

BETTER COMMUNICATION

The lack of adequate communication links became painfully obvious during March 1996. Only when the crisis was under way did Anthony Lake, President Clinton's national security adviser, manage to open an authoritative back channel with his Chinese equivalent, Liu Huaqiu, the director of the State Council's Foreign Affairs Office, who happened to be on a previously scheduled visit to Washington at the time (Gellman 1998). Although Presidents Clinton and Jiang agreed to establish a hotline during their 1997 summit, this proved to be of little use in the aftermath of the May 8, 1999, bombing of the Chinese embassy in Belgrade, when Jiang initially refused to take Clinton's calls (Mann 1999a). At the worst moments in their relationship, Beijing and Washington have had to improvise, or do without, the kind of communication channels that can be essential for limiting a crisis.

In addition to hotlines, all sides need to improve and expand routine political and military exchanges. At the top, the China-U.S. relationship has suffered from a lack of regular summit visits, which give leaders on both sides a chance to discuss their respective interests in the Taiwan Strait. President Clinton did not visit China until halfway through his second term in office. On this score, China and Japan have been more successful in maintaining regular top-level contact, with seven summits since 1990.[6]

Lack of momentum at the top has hindered the development of military-to-military ties. Joseph W. Prueher, the U.S. ambassador to China (into 2001) and former commander-in-chief of U.S. forces in the Pacific, lamented in 1998 that military exchanges between China and the United States are too formalized with little interaction between mid- and lower-level officers.[7] Contact between the PLA and Japan's Self-Defense Forces has followed a similar model, though Beijing and Tokyo have taken steps in recent years to deepen their military-to-military relations.[8] Although more and better political and military exchanges will not magically solve the deep divisions between China, Japan, and the United States over Taiwan, they can help build mutual trust and help China better understand Japanese and U.S. security policies, and vice versa.

Some form of trilateral dialogue between China, Japan, and the United States may also prove useful. For Japanese and American leaders, such talks would offer an opportunity to convince China that the Japan-U.S. alliance does not exist for the purpose of perpetuating Taiwan's separation and to encourage China to exercise restraint in its military buildup. China, meanwhile, would likely use such talks to gain further assurances from Tokyo and Washington that they will not support Taiwanese independence. Because official trilateral discussions may not be feasible in the near term, unofficial track-two dialogues can also play an important role in managing the Taiwan issue. China has participated in track-two initiatives among scholars, foreign policy experts, and former officials to discuss developments across the Taiwan Strait. In general, China does not object to Taiwan's participation in such exchanges. One such project, sponsored by the New York–based National Committee on U.S. Foreign Policy, involves discussions between influential academics and policy experts from China, Taiwan, and the United States. Some incumbent U.S. officials have participated in these discussions (Fu 1999). The Japan Center for International Exchange has sponsored similar track-two efforts between China, Japan, and the United States. In addition to offering an opportunity for Taiwanese participation, track-two programs could help pave the way for official track-one discussions.

MORE AND BETTER
CROSS-STRAIT POLITICAL DIALOGUE

The risk of another Taiwan crisis is all the greater because Beijing and Taipei have yet to establish an effective dialogue mechanism. In 1992, the two sides inaugurated quasi-official talks between Taipei's Straits Exchange Foundation (SEF) and Beijing's Association for Relations across the Taiwan Strait (ARATS), two "white glove" organizations that allow the two sides to interact, while technically avoiding official contact. However, even after eight years, Beijing and Taipei have failed to make headway on a modest agenda of functional issues such as fishing disputes and the repatriation of illegal immigrants. The talks have been as fragile as they have been unproductive. In 1995, China halted the dialogue following Lee's trip to Cornell and talks did not resume until the October 1998 visit of SEF Chairman Koo Chen-fu to China. Talks were again suspended indefinitely after Lee's "special state-to-state" remark and as of August 2000 had not yet restarted.

All in all, the SEF-ARATS channel has failed to enhance security in the Taiwan Strait. China urges that talks on political, as well as functional, issues are needed and Taiwan has agreed in principle, yet both sides have set preconditions that the other categorically rejects; Taipei is unwilling to accept subequal status under Beijing's version of "one China," whereas Beijing is just as unwilling to deal with Taipei on any basis that might imply Taiwan is a separate sovereignty.

Events in the first half of 2000 offered some hope that this impasse might be broken. In its white paper on Taiwan policy issued February 21, the Chinese government expressed a willingness to deal with Taiwan on the "basis of equality" and proposed that such talks could be conducted between political parties (Information Office of the State Council 2000). The change in leadership in Taipei also raises the possibility of new breakthroughs in cross-strait relations. Chen has compared himself to Richard Nixon. A bona fide Taiwanese nationalist, Chen claims he can be trusted to negotiate with China without selling out Taiwan's interests, much as the stridently anti-communist Nixon was able to bargain with China (Pomfret 2000). Chen has made a number of bold proposals aimed at restarting a dialogue. Following his election, he offered to travel to mainland

China for a "peace summit" prior to his inauguration. Chen's administration has also prioritized the establishment of direct trade, transport, and communications (the "mini three links") between the Taiwan-controlled islands of Kinmen and Matsu as an intermediate step toward establishing broader direct contacts across the entire Taiwan Strait. In July 2000, he called for the two sides to return to the "spirit of 1992"—the year semiofficial cross-strait talks began—by simply shelving disagreements over "one China" and working to expand exchanges. As of this writing, however, such proposals have failed to illicit a positive response from China. Differences over the meaning of "one China"—Taiwan prefers a cultural/ethnic definition, whereas China stresses a political "one China" with only one sovereignty—will continue to be the primary barrier to meaningful cross-strait dialogue.

MAKING REUNIFICATION MORE ATTRACTIVE TO THE PEOPLE OF TAIWAN

China's threat to use force has convinced most on Taiwan that pursuit of de jure independence is not a viable option. This is evidenced both in the DPP's moderation of its once strongly pro-independence position and the weak levels of support for hard-line independence groups such as the Taiwan Independence Party (which received just under 1.5 percent of the vote in the 1998 parliamentary elections and was unable to even place its candidate on the ballot in the March 2000 presidential contest). However, mainland China's saber rattling has profoundly alienated the people of Taiwan from the Chinese government. Although China's deterrence-focused approach has decreased the appeal of a separate Taiwanese republic, Beijing has failed miserably in convincing the people of Taiwan that early reunification is in their best interest.

If anything, China's image on Taiwan is growing worse. Taiwan's recent steps away from the "one China" principle reflect the island's deep dissatisfaction with China's efforts to isolate Taipei on the world stage. Beijing's attempt to keep Taiwan from participating as a non-state member of the World Trade Organization (at least until China is admitted first) and the World Health Organization reinforces the common sentiment in Taiwan that China cares more about the dip-lomatic scorecard than the welfare of Taiwan's people. The depth of Taiwanese distrust of China was seen in the aftermath of the earth-quake that struck Taiwan on September 21, 1999. China's requests for international aid on Taiwan's behalf, under the pretext that Beijing is the "central government," and demands that any UN relief efforts be initiated by Beijing ("Mainland Works to Help" 1999) angered Tai-wanese leaders who accused China of crassly using the disaster to score political points.

The fact that Beijing has achieved almost total victory in its dip-lomatic battle with Taipei should give the Chinese authorities the confidence to give Taiwan more space as a substate participant in the international community. Returning to a more conciliatory policy emphasizing negotiation and Beijing's desire not to use force, while simultaneously accelerating the process of democratization on the mainland, is probably the best way for the Chinese government to improve its image among the Taiwanese public.

PUSHING BACK CHINA'S TIME HORIZON

The situation in the Taiwan Strait is unlikely to stabilize unless China can be confident that its window of opportunity to reunify with Tai-wan is not closing. Taiwan's seeming abandonment of "one China" has reinforced the belief among Chinese leaders that reunification must happen soon, if it is to happen at all. China has drawn a line in the sand by demanding that Taiwan not revise its constitution to in-clude "special state-to-state," which Chen has promised not to do. The risk is that Taiwan, as it takes incremental steps to establish its equality and separate sovereignty, will finally push China into a cor-ner where Beijing believes it has no choice but to use force. Because it is no longer clear where the independence "trip wire" now lies, Taiwan will need to proceed with caution as it reforms its bloated political system inherited from the KMT. The 1997 decision to "freeze" rather than "abolish" the Taiwan provincial government—a redundant level of bureaucracy but also a significant symbol of Tai-wan's connection to the mainland—is an example of the ambiguity Taiwan must maintain to avoid provoking Beijing.

DISCOURAGING MILITARIZATION OF
THE TAIWAN ISSUE

Much, but not all, of the responsibility for demilitarizing the Taiwan issue lies with Beijing. In addition to alienating the Taiwanese, China's military displays and missile deployments have boosted support in Japan and the United States for a more robust American military presence in the region, more arms sales to Taiwan, and Taiwan's inclusion in TMD—all of which China perceives as counter to its interests.

Japan and the United States must maintain a delicate balance between effectively deterring any use of force in the Taiwan Strait and being overly provocative toward China. Some proposals in the U.S. Congress to vastly expand the levels of Taiwan-U.S. military cooperation—such as the Taiwan Security Enhancement Act[9]—could actually work to reduce Taiwan's overall security by encouraging a greater military buildup by mainland China. Although the United States is obligated under the Taiwan Relations Act to continue sales of defensive weapons to Taiwan, these sales should be made in light of the PLA's actual capabilities (which are improving but still limited) rather than hypothetical, alarmist projections of China's future military power. Also, as stated in the 1982 Sino-American Joint Communiqué, China's commitment to a peaceful resolution should be taken into account, meaning the United States should be prepared to scale back weapons sales in accordance with the communiqué if China halts its military intimidation of Taiwan, or, better yet, renounces the use of force altogether.

TMD presents a particularly difficult dilemma for Tokyo and Washington, even though any TMD system is years away from actual deployment. Japan and the United States should explore ways of providing Taiwan with a missile defense that falls short of making Taiwan a de facto alliance partner. From a military standpoint, given Taiwan's small geographic area and proximity to mainland China, it may make more sense for Taiwan to concentrate on developing a self-contained lower-tier missile defense system rather than participate in an expensive regionwide TMD network. The United States is already supplying Taiwan with low-altitude missile defense equipment such as the Patriot missile. Another possibility would be for the United

States to deploy mobile, sea-based missile defense systems that could provide protection for Taiwan yet remain under American control.

CONCLUSION

The ongoing dispute between Beijing and Taipei will continue to hinder China-Japan-U.S. trilateral relations for the foreseeable future. Although the election of a new president in Taiwan raises the possibility of improved cross-strait ties, the difficulties between the two sides are not simply the result of individuals but rather the widening political gap between Taiwan and the mainland. China and Taiwan want to settle their dispute without outside intermediaries, but Beijing and Taipei have so far failed to establish a robust dialogue mechanism for effectively handling their differences. At the beginning of the new millennium, both sides seem to realize that political discussions, rather than just functional talks, are needed to break the present impasse. Actually starting such political talks, though, will require flexibility and compromise, two things that have been in short supply on both sides of the Taiwan Strait. However, given the shared desire of Beijing and Taipei to avoid a military confrontation, especially when both are enjoying unprecedented economic success (thanks in no small part to cross-strait trade and investment links), chances seem good that if given enough time the two sides will succeed in reducing hostility and, in the long run, find a permanent solution. But for such time to be available the status quo must remain viable.

Hence, it is not up to America and Japan to "solve" the Taiwan problem. Rather, Tokyo and Washington should concentrate on creating an atmosphere conducive to productive Beijing-Taipei relations. To do so, Japan and the United States should emphasize their shared interest in a peaceful settlement, but should avoid taking positions on what such a settlement should look like. If Taiwan perceives Japan and the United States as endorsing China's view of "one country, two systems," Taipei will likely grow more assertive in seeking recognition as a separate state. Simultaneously, if China views Japan and the United States as encouraging Taiwanese independence, Beijing will have more incentives to attempt a unilateral solution lest Taiwan slip away forever. Maintaining neutrality in the cross-strait political dispute under a "one China, peaceful solution" policy should remain a central pillar of American and Japanese foreign policy. Above all, China must be convinced that stability, not the independence of Taiwan, is the ultimate goal of the expanded Japan-U.S. security alliance.

China, Japan, and the United States should also be careful not to exaggerate the "Taiwan dividend." Although it is true that a peaceful solution to the Taiwan issue would remove a major source of irritation in Japan-China and China-U.S. ties, resolution of the cross-strait dispute would not by itself guarantee a fundamental improvement of trilateral relations. Many of the subplots of the Taiwan issue—including Beijing's bitterness over past humiliations, the lack of Sino-Japanese postwar reconciliation, and China's opposition to American hegemony—will likely continue, even after the Taiwan problem is solved. Also, Japan and the United States still have anxieties about the impact of a rising China on regional and global security, concerns that are largely independent of whether Taiwan and mainland China reunify. China, Japan, and the United States must continue to try to work through these underlying problems even as a solution to the more narrow issue of Taiwan remains elusive. Otherwise, a breakthrough in cross-strait relations, rather than promoting greater cooperation, may only serve to bring to the forefront more serious conflicts between China, Japan, and the United States over the future leadership of the East Asian region and China's place in the global order of the twenty-first century.

NOTES

1. Taiwan officially adopted this formula on August 1, 1992, when the National Unification Council passed its "Resolution on the Meaning of 'One China'" (http://www.gov.tw/english/MacPolicy/policy3/chinae.htm).

2. Several prominent Taiwanese business leaders have criticized Taipei's "no haste, be patient" policy designed to limit cross-strait economic interdependence. For example, Y. C. Wang, the chairman of the Formosa Plastics Group, has argued that Taiwan should enter into a confederation with China under the "one-China" principle as a way to reduce cross-strait tensions (see Yeh 1997). Also, the American Chamber of Commerce in Taipei's 1997–1998 *Taiwan White Paper* is critical of the Taiwan government's efforts to limit cross-strait economic interaction (see "Amcham's Taiwan Report" 1997).

3. On August 17, 1997, Japanese Chief Cabinet Secretary Kajiyama Seiroku stated in a television interview that the geographic scope of the alliance—referred to in the defense guidelines as simply the "areas surrounding Japan"—includes Taiwan. And in January 1999 Ozawa Ichirō, the head of Japan's Liberal Party (then part of the ruling coalition) angered China with a similar remark (He 1999; Kristof 1997).

4. Jiang's eight points were (1) adherence to "one China," (2) Taiwan can pursue nongovernmental economic and cultural ties to other countries and international organizations, (3) China is willing to open negotiations with Taiwanese political parties and "mass organizations," (4) "Chinese should not fight fellow Chinese," (5) cross-strait trade and economic cooperation should be expanded, (6) Chinese on both sides of the Taiwan Strait are the inheritors of Chinese culture, (7) China should work to protect the rights and interests of the Taiwanese, and (8) China welcomes Taiwanese leaders to visit the mainland (see "President Jiang's Speech" 1995).

5. See the address by Sha Zukang, director-general of the Department of Arms Control and Disarmament at China's Ministry of Foreign Affairs, to the Seventh Carnegie International Non-Proliferation Conference on January 12, 1999 (reprinted in Ming 1999, 75–80). Sha says, "If a country, in addition to its offensive power, seeks to develop advanced TMD or even NMD [national missile defense] in an attempt to attain absolute security and unilateral strategic advantage for itself, other countries will be forced to develop more advanced offensive missiles. This will give rise to a new round of arms race which will be in no one's interest" (79).

6. Five Japanese prime ministers have visited China since 1990—Kaifu Toshiki (August 10–13, 1991), Hosokawa Morihiro (March 19–21, 1994), Murayama Tomiichi (May 3, 1995), Hashimoto Ryūtarō (September 4, 1997), and Obuchi Keizō (July 8–10, 1999). Jiang Zemin visited Japan twice in April 1992 (as CCP secretary general) and again in November 1998 (as China's president).

7. In a speech at Fudan University in Shanghai on November 13, 1998, Admiral Joseph W. Prueher stated that "we want to develop and increase understanding by moving our military relationship beyond the very senior policy, foreign affairs and protocol channels and into more routine operational channels. Today, I must pass through several layers of bureaucracy to speak directly with senior PLA officers—it is not an easy process. With other nations in the region, it is a simple process to telephone my colleagues in the military to discuss matters of mutual concern. Our U.S.-China relationship is now robust enough to sustain this type of operational contact" (Prueher 1999, 170).

8. Despite differences over the expanded Japan-U.S. alliance, Beijing and Tokyo have increased contacts among military leaders and civilian defense officials. In February 1998, General Chi Haotian, China's minister of national defense, visited Japan. This was the first official visit by a Chinese defense minister to Japan (Defense Minister Zhang Aiping made a private trip to Tokyo in 1984). During Chi's visit, China agreed to reciprocal visits by the Chief of the PLA General Staff Fu Quanyou and Japanese Joint Staff Council Chairman Natsukawa Kazuya. Japan's ground forces chief of staff, Fujinawa Yūji, visited Beijing in March 1998 and Zhang Wannian, the vice chairman of China's Central Military Commission, made an unofficial stopover

visit to Japan in September of that same year (Zhang was on his way back from the United States). The visit by Fu, however, was delayed. In November 1999, China and Japan agreed to have Fu visit Japan in the first half of 2000.

9. The Senate version (S. 693) of the act was submitted on March 24, 1999, with Jesse Helms (R-N.C.) and Robert Torricelli (D-N.J.) as cosponsors. The House version (H.R. 1838) was introduced on May 18, 1999, cosponsored by Thomas Delay (R-Texas), Robert Andrews (D-N.J.), Benjamin Gilman (R-N.Y.), Peter Deutsch (D-Fla.), Dana Rohrabacher (R-Calif.), David Wu (D-Ore.), Christopher Cox (R-Calif.), William Jefferson (D-La.), Lincoln Daiz-Balart (R-Fla.), Nita Lowey (D-N.Y.), Christopher Smith (R-N.J.), Duncan Hunter (R-Calif.), Dan Burton (R-Ind.), Merrill Cook (R-Utah), and David Weldon (R-Fla.).

Bibliography

Albright, David, and Corey Gay. 1998. "Taiwan: Nuclear Nightmare Averted." *The Bulletin of the Atomic Scientists* 54(1). <http://www.bullatomsci.org/issues/1998/ jf98/jf98albright.html> (September 1999).
"Amcham's Taiwan Report Presented in Washington." 1997. *China News* (Taipei). 27 September. Online. Lexis-Nexis. (September 1999).
Baum, Julian. 1999. "Dangerous Liaisons." *Far Eastern Economic Review* 162(12): 10.
Blair, Admiral Dennis. 2000. "Speech to the Carnegie Endowment for International Peace Nonproliferation Conference." Federal News Service. 16 March. Online. Lexis-Nexis. (May 2000).
Bodeen, Christopher. 1999. "Taiwan's Vice President Urges Long-Range Missile Development." Associated Press. 8 December. Online. Lexis-Nexis. (June 2000).
Chang Yi-fan. 1999. "No Intervention in China's International Affairs under Pretext of Taiwan Issue Is Tolerated—Interviewing Chinese Ambassador to Japan Chen Jian." *Hong Kong Economic Journal* (Hong Kong Hsin Pao). 13 August. In Foreign Broadcast Information Service (FBIS) Daily Report, 13 August (FBIS-CHI-1999-0814).
Chen Shui-bian. 2000. "Taiwan Stands Up: Advancing to an Uplifting Era." Inaugural address. 20 May. <http://www.oop.gov.tw/english2000/2000520/speech .htm> (June 2000).
Cheng Siyi. 2000. "One China Principle Cannot Be Shaken: Criticize Lu Xiulian's 'Taiwan Independence' Fallacy" (in Chinese). *People's Liberation Army Daily* (15 April). <http://www.pladaily.com.cn/html/2000/04/15/a20000415_02.htm> (June 2000)
Fu Yi-jie. 1999. "Round Table Discussions Underway Today, U.S. Military Officials Participate for First Time" (in Chinese). *Shijie ribao* (World journal) (30 August): A1.
Gellman, Barton. 1998. "U.S. and China Nearly Came to Blows in '96; Tension over Taiwan Prompted Repair of Ties." *Washington Post* (21 June): A1. Online. Lexis-Nexis. (September 1999).
Government Information Office (Taipei). 1999. "President Lee's Responses to

Questions Submitted by *Deutsche Welle.*" 9 July. <http://www.gio.gov.tw/info/99html/99lee/0709.htm> (September 1999).

He Cong. 1999. "Japan's Right-Turn Tendency as Seen from Ozawa's Crazy Remarks." Zhong guo tongxun she (China News Agency). 23 January. As translated in Foreign Broadcast Information Service (FBIS) Daily Report, 27 January (FBIS-CHI-99-027).

Information Office of the State Council. 2000. "The One-China Principle and the Taiwan Issue." Reprinted in *China Daily* (22 February): 4–5.

International Institute for Strategic Studies. 1999. *The Military Balance 1999/2000.* Oxford, England: International Institute for Strategic Studies.

"Japanese MPs to Push for Taiwanese President Lee's Visit to Japan." 1995. Agence France Presse. 15 June.

Jiang Zemin. 1999. "Speech to Rally in Beijing in Celebration of Macao's Return to China." Xinhua News Agency (English). 20 December. Online. Lexis-Nexis. (June 2000).

Kristof, Nicholas D. 1997. "For Japan, a Quandary on Pleasing Two Giants." *New York Times* (24 August): A9.

Lam, Willy Wo-lap. 1999. *The Era of Jiang Zemin.* Singapore: Prentice Hall, Inc.

Lee Teng-hui. 1999. *Taiwan de zhuzhang* (Taiwan's viewpoint). Taipei, Taiwan: Yuan-Liou Publishing Co., Ltd.

Mainland Affairs Council (Taipei). 1999a. *Liang an jingji tongji yue bao* (Cross-strait economic statistics monthly) 78(February): 24.

———. 1999b. "Parity, Peace, and Win-Win: The Republic of China's Position on the 'Special State-to-State' Relationship." 1 August. <http://www.mac.gov.tw/english/macpolicy/policy17/880803.htm> (September 1999).

———. 2000. Public opinion survey. <http://www.mac.gov.tw/english/POS/890623/8906e_b.htm> (June 2000).

"Mainland Works to Help Quake Victims." 1999. *China Daily.* 21 October. Online. Lexis-Nexis. (June 2000).

Mann, Jim. 1999a. "Hotline between China, U.S. Runs Cold in Crisis." *Los Angeles Times* (12 May): A5.

———. 1999b. "U.S. Attempt to Draw China, Taiwan into Talks Backfires." *Los Angeles Times* (10 October): A1.

———. 1999c. "U.S. Has Secretly Expanded Military Ties with Taiwan." *Los Angeles Times* (24 July): A1.

Ming Zhang. 1999. *China's Changing Nuclear Posture.* Washington, D.C.: Carnegie Endowment for International Peace.

Moore, Jonathan. 1999. "The Smoke Clears in the Noodle Wars." *Business Week* (International ed.) (3633): 28.

Office of the President. 2000. "Transcript of Presidential Press Conference." 20 June. <http://www.oop.gov.tw/english2000/news/index.htm> (June 2000).

Pomfret, John. 2000. "A Vote Beyond Its Borders; Taiwan Election Critical to China Relations; Regional Economy." *Washington Post* (18 March): A13.

"President Jiang's Speech on Reunification." 1995. BBC Summary of World Broadcasts. 31 January. Online. Lexis-Nexis. (September 1999).

Prueher, Joseph W. 1999. "Asia-Pacific Security and China." *Vital Speeches of the Day* 65(6): 167–170.

"Re-definition of China Ties 'Product of Careful Study.'" 1999. *China News* (Taipei). 14 July. Online. Lexis-Nexis. (September 1999).

Sha Zukang. 1999. Address to the Seventh Carnegie International Non-Proliferation Conference. 12 January. Reprinted in Ming Zhang. 1999. *China's Changing Nuclear Posture*. Washington, D.C.: Carnegie Endowment for International Peace.

Sims, Calvin. 1999. "U.S. and Japan Agree to Joint Research on Missile Defense." *New York Times* (17 August): A4.

"Taiwan Has No Plans to Resume Nuclear Weapons Development: Lee." 1995. Agence France Presse. 28 July. Online. Lexis-Nexis. (September 1999).

"Tokyo Governor's Pro-Tibet, Taiwan Remarks Raise Ire of China Media." 1999. Agence France Presse. 18 April. Online. Lexis-Nexis. (September 1999).

Tung Chen-yuan. 1999. "Trilateral Economic Relations among Taiwan, China, and the United States." *Asian Affairs* 25(4): 220–235.

Unsigned editorial. 1999. "Yaohai shi pohuai yi ge zhongguo de yuanze" (Crucial point is to destroy one China principle). *People's Daily* (14 July): 1.

Wang Flor. 1999. "MND [Ministry of National Defense] Warns Taiwan of Beijing's Information War." Central News Agency (Taipei). 10 August. Online. Lexis-Nexis. (September 1999).

White House Office of the Press Secretary. 1998. "Remarks by the President and First Lady in Discussion on Shaping China for the 21st Century." 30 June.

Yates, Stephen J. 1998. "Clinton Statement Undermines Taiwan." Heritage Foundation Executive Memorandum, no. 538. 10 July. <www.heritage.org/library/execmemo/em538.html> (September 1999).

Yeh, Benjamin. 1997. "Taiwanese Mogul Paints Picture of Chinese Confederation." Agence France Presse. 14 September. Online. Lexis-Nexis. (September 1999).

III ⚓ Defense or Security? The U.S.-Japan Defense Guidelines and China

Michael J. Green

IN THEIR RECENT HISTORIES of World War I, John Keegan, Byron Farwell, and Niall Ferguson all agree on one point (Farwell 1999; Ferguson 1999; Keegan 1999). The war erupted at a time of unprecedented economic interdependence in Europe primarily because defense planners in France, Russia, and Germany felt compelled to implement military mobilization schedules to prevent potential adversaries from gaining the advantage by mobilizing first. Diplomats, industrialists, and monarchs who had held together a prosperous Europe and averted earlier confrontations became prisoners to the tyranny of the military planners' inflexible timetables. More than nine million died in a war that started because states pursued defense instead of security.

Critics of the reaffirmation of the Japan-U.S. alliance in the 1990s make a similar charge. They argue that the search for a defense against missiles and the implementation of bilateral defense planning for regional contingencies might improve the defensive capabilities of Japan and the United States but at the cost of overall security in East Asia. These critics assert that multipolarity and economic interdependence in East Asia should be encouraged instead. They charge that the Japan-U.S. alliance is, in fact, expanding at the cost of other states' interests in the region. This perspective is particularly strong in China.

Given the violent history of Sino-Japanese relations and the potential for confrontation with the United States over Taiwan, China has reason to be concerned about any changes in the Japan-U.S. alliance. Yet China also continues to benefit from the stability provided by Japan's alignment with the United States. A disintegration of the Japan-U.S. alliance would create unacceptable levels of uncertainty

73

in the region; China would have to assume that Japan and, therefore, North Korea would acquire nuclear weapons and expand their offensive capabilities. Multipolarity is good, in theory, but not if one's immediate neighbors become nuclear-armed poles as a consequence.

The revitalization of the Japan-U.S. alliance beginning in 1995–1996 aimed to enhance the Japan-U.S. common defense and to stabilize regional security. Its purpose was to reestablish reliability and credibility to bilateral security relations at a time of strategic flux in the region, and following questions about the Japanese and U.S. commitment to the alliance itself. Rather than expand the alliance, the revitalization initiative aimed to restore it. Alliance managers on both sides of the Pacific proceeded with the knowledge that a substantive change in the division of military roles and missions between Japan and the United States (since the 1980s with the United States as the "spear" and Japan as the "shield") would undermine rather than enhance regional security—and so they avoided such a change. But they also recognized that the alliance might not survive a security crisis on the Korean peninsula without some higher level of bilateral planning within the framework provided by the division of roles and missions. The political credibility of the alliance, therefore, depended on its operational credibility.

Rather than change the status quo, Japan and the United States were attempting to maintain it. Nevertheless, because the Japanese and U.S. objectives are simultaneously defense and security, attention must be given to Chinese concerns. In some areas, constraints on the alliance should be clarified. In other areas, Chinese criticism cannot be justified by the actual state of Japan-U.S. defense cooperation. If China's objective is to maintain the status quo, then Japan and the United States can reinvigorate the alliance in a way that does so. If, however, China objects to a continuation of the status quo, then those in Japan and the United States who argue that China is a "strategic competitor" will prevail and the Japan-U.S. alliance may well change or expand in more fundamental ways.

Others can explain China's strategic intentions in East Asia. In this chapter, I will describe the motivations behind the reaffirmation of the Japan-U.S. alliance in the mid-1990s and, specifically, the revision of the Guidelines for U.S.-Japan Defense Cooperation. Like the Japanese film *Rashōmon*, descriptions of the revision process vary to a large extent depending on the position of the observer. Some excellent histories have been written by journalists and scholars, most notably Funabashi Yōichi's *Alliance Adrift* (1999). Descriptive essays have also been published by Pentagon officials (Giarra 1997). I was in an advantageous position to follow the debates and discussions that led to the April 1996 Japan-U.S. Joint Security Declaration, which initiated the review of the Defense Guidelines and signaled Japan's interest in theater missile defense (TMD).* Although this is not intended as an authoritative account of those events, I will describe the objectives, obstacles, and pressures in the alliance that led to the Joint Security Declaration and, specifically, how the Defense Guidelines fit. Then I will proceed to review Chinese concerns and suggest proposals for enhancing the Japan-U.S. defense relationship in ways that should not threaten Chinese security interests, so that Japan and the United States can enjoy a strong defense and the entire region enhanced security.

THE STRATEGIC CONTEXT

The end of the cold war signaled that Japan and the United States should redefine their security policy into more comprehensive terms than the narrow strategy of containment. After the 1991 Gulf War in which important constituencies in Japan and the United States were dissatisfied with the degree, scope, and nature of Japanese participation, Tokyo and Washington began experimenting with new definitions of security, while neglecting the bilateral alliance. By the mid-1990s, however, it became clear in both countries that the alliance relationship needed attention. The drift in bilateral security relations from 1992 to 1996 and the reemergence of security problems in Asia explain the broader strategic context behind the reaffirmation of the Japan-U.S. alliance and the revision of the Defense Guidelines.

The drift in Japan-U.S. security relations began in the final year of George Bush's administration. Flush with victory in the Gulf and

I was an analyst at the Institute for Defense Analyses (1995–1996) and adviser to the Office of Asia Pacific Affairs in the Department of Defense (1996–1997). This essay is not intended to represent the official positions of either institution.

eager to cash in security expertise for credibility on economic policy, the president used his January 1992 summit in Tokyo to highlight trade problems with Japan by inviting the corporate executive officers of the major American auto companies to accompany him. This gimmick backfired politically in the United States and in building bilateral relations with Japan, and the summit became most memorable for the president vomiting in the lap of Prime Minister Miyazawa Kiichi at a state dinner. Whereas Bush toyed with alliance relations to win confidence in his economic policies, Bill Clinton entered office in 1993 with an ideological outlook that placed economics at the center of security relations with Japan. As Robert Uriu (2000) demonstrates in his new study of Clinton's Japan policy, the new administration accepted (without criticism) the arguments of revisionists who argued that Japan was developing a separate definition of national security strategy based on technological and economic development. Mobilized by this revisionist view of Japan, the administration spent its first three years pressing the Japanese government for results-oriented trade agreements and greater reciprocity in dual-use technology flows. Neither initiative produced significant results, but they did alienate important friends of the Japan-U.S. alliance in Tokyo.

In Japan, the end of the cold war, the growing economic integration of Asia, and the conflict in the Gulf spurred a search for new approaches to security. In 1993, Prime Minister Hosokawa Morihiro established a blue ribbon panel to deliberate on the future of Japanese security policy under the leadership of Asahi Beer Chairman Higuchi Hirotaro. In its final report in 1994, the Higuchi Commission recommended a three-pronged Japanese approach to security: (1) multilateralism, (2) the Japan-U.S. alliance, and (3) independent self-defense capabilities (Cronin and Green 1994). Of these, multilateralism was imbued with great importance as the new look in Japanese security policy. The Gulf War—a UN-sanctioned, multinational effort—had left the Japanese political leadership with a profound sense of impotence in international affairs. After the Gulf War, Japan began a concerted bid for permanent membership in the UN Security Council, passed legislation authorizing limited participation in UN peacekeeping operations, and pushed for the creation of multilateral security forums in East Asia. These reforms did not suggest the abandonment of the Japan-U.S. alliance but rather a new departure for Japan to play a larger role in international security affairs. This theme figured prominently in early drafts of the Japan Defense Agency's new National Defense Program Outline (NDPO), a revised version of the original 1976 document and the blueprint for future Japanese defense planning.

The Japanese and U.S. experiments with new approaches to security were not out of sync with changes in the structure of international relations after the cold war. However, the emphasis on multilateral security in Tokyo and economic security in Washington created mutual unease. Meanwhile, key aspects of the security relationship lay in disrepair. The consequences of this situation became apparent to both governments in the spring of 1994. In April of that year, the State Department was warned by every U.S. ambassador in East Asia that the region expected American political and military withdrawal (Williams and Chandler 1994). That same month, the crisis with North Korea over its suspected nuclear facilities forced Japan and the United States to refocus on pure military-to-military cooperation. During the last decade of the cold war, the United States had come to expect Japanese support in the event of a major war in Asia. The commander of the U.S. Seventh Fleet asked his Japanese counterpart for logistical support and minesweepers in the event that the United Nations approved an embargo on North Korea; this was not the Gulf, after all, but Japan's backyard. However, the Japanese response was negative. There was no legal formula for Japan to provide operational support to the United States. During the cold war, the premise had been a Soviet attack on Japan, not an embargo. Prime Minister Hata Tsutomu promised that once a crisis occurred, he would do his best to pass legislation allowing action, but that was a thin reed on which to plan for real military confrontation.

The general drift in the alliance was now given specific form. It was clear that despite broad support for continued alliance relations in Japan and the United States, each country had lost credibility with the other. An alliance relationship cannot survive under such circumstances, particularly when faced with a crisis. Thus, in late 1994, the Japanese and U.S. governments formally launched what was soon dubbed in the press as "the Nye Initiative" after Assistant Secretary of Defense Joseph Nye. In general terms, the purpose was to demonstrate the Japanese and U.S. commitments to the alliance and to the U.S. forward military presence in East Asia. The two governments consulted on a series of policy documents to achieve this goal:

- The February 1995 Department of Defense *East Asian Strategic Report* (EASR) emphasized the U.S. intent to maintain approximately 100,000 U.S. troops in Asia for the foreseeable future.
- Japan's November 1995 revised National Defense Program Outline introduced peacekeeping as a theme for Japanese defense policy but highlighted in eleven places the centrality of the Japan-U.S. alliance to Japanese security. The document basically redefined Japan's basic defense requirement from "defense against small-scale limited attack" to "responding to situations that arise in the area around Japan that have a direct effect on Japanese security"—based on the Japan-U.S. alliance and the constraints imposed by the Japanese constitution.
- In the April 1996 Joint Security Declaration, President Clinton and Prime Minister Hashimoto Ryūtarō reaffirmed the Japan-U.S. alliance and asked their governments to initiate a revision of the 1978 Defense Guidelines.

Throughout this process, China was a constant factor in alliance managers' thinking but never the central reason for the reaffirmation of the alliance or the revision of the Defense Guidelines. Rather, military planners were focused on shoring up defense cooperation with an eye to the Korean peninsula. Policymakers focused on stabilizing bilateral political relations, particularly after the crisis caused in September 1995 when three U.S. military personnel raped a young Japanese girl in Okinawa. At the strategic level, many Americans recognized the need for a stable Japan-U.S. alignment—not to contain China but to integrate China into a predictable and secure Asia Pacific community. The Japanese side was much more apprehensive about the China dimension of the alliance reaffirmation. Japanese irritation with China grew after the 1995 Chinese nuclear tests, but the government of Murayama Tomiichi was reluctant to even include the term *China* in early drafts of the Joint Security Declaration for fear that Beijing might misunderstand Japanese intentions.

The Joint Security Declaration was planned for the Clinton-Murayama summit in November 1995, on the wings of the Asia-Pacific

Economic Cooperation (APEC) forum summit in Osaka. However, President Clinton postponed the summit until April 1996 so that he could attend to a domestic political crisis over the federal budget. That lag of five months made an enormous difference in the politics and perceptions of the Joint Security Declaration for a number of reasons. First, in January 1996, Hashimoto, a pro-defense leader in the Liberal Democratic Party, replaced the Socialist Murayama as prime minister. Then, in March, China bracketed Taiwan with missiles, and the United States responded by deploying two carriers—one from Japan—to signal its displeasure and reassure friends and allies in the region and elsewhere. To many in China, by April 1996 the Joint Security Declaration seemed aimed at Beijing. Meanwhile, to a majority of politicians in Japan, Chinese actions provided one more source of uncertainty about the future of East Asian security without an alliance with the United States. Beijing now viewed specific policies initiated in the Joint Security Declaration—especially the review of the Defense Guidelines and later joint collaboration on TMD— as litmus tests on whether the renewed alliance would be aimed at China. In Tokyo and Washington, Beijing's mounting objections to the Defense Guidelines reinforced burgeoning suspicions that China intended to change the status quo in Asia, not to maintain it.

The U.S.-Japan Defense Guidelines

The original Guidelines for U.S.–Japan Defense Cooperation were signed in 1978, two years after Tokyo's first NDPO. The NDPO had quieted a decade of debate about the level of independent Japanese defense capabilities by declaring that Japan would rely on the Japan-U.S. alliance and only build up the military power necessary to cope with "direct small-scale limited invasions." In the Guidelines, Tokyo hoped to reinforce the political credibility of the new NDPO by authorizing planning with the U.S. forces for the defense of Japan. The U.S. government supported this goal but also hoped to lock in a Japanese commitment to provide rear-area logistical support for U.S. forces in the event of a conflict in the region. In 1969, Prime Minister Satō Eisaku had promised President Richard Nixon, in the famous "Satō-Nixon communiqué," that the security of Taiwan and

South Korea were important to Japan. With Sino-U.S. relations improving, Taiwan did not matter per se, but the U.S. government did want Japan to begin planning with the United States for the defense of South Korea. From the moment Satō agreed to the 1969 communiqué, however, Tokyo resisted, believing that Satō had uttered the reference to Taiwanese and South Korean security only to achieve the return of Okinawa to Japanese sovereignty—which he did.

In the 1980s, this distinction between the narrow defense of Japan and a security role in the region was blurred by the Soviet military buildup in the Far East. Japan, by defending its own immediate territory and sea lanes (out to 1,000 nautical miles), was now a de facto frontline state and regional security player in the military standoff with the Soviet Union. Japanese and American forces trained for joint missions in antisubmarine warfare, minesweeping, and air defense in the waters around Japan—effectively bottling up Soviet forces aimed at the whole region—but the premise remained the same: the defense of Japan. Of course, that whole convenient arrangement collapsed along with the Soviet Union.

It was not until the Gulf War—and, more acutely, the North Korean nuclear crisis of 1994—that the U.S. government recognized how dependent its military cooperation had become on the premise of a direct Soviet attack on Japan. As U.S. planners prepared responses to the North Korean nuclear provocation (including such options as a blockade), the Japanese government did not know if it could offer support absent a precipitating direct attack on Japan. This, after, all, had been the premise that allowed regional defense cooperation in the territory around Japan during the cold war. But in the Korean crisis of 1994, Tokyo lacked the clear and present danger that the Soviets had provided with their aggressive expansion in the 1980s. Did the North Korean nuclear program represent a direct military threat to the Japanese home territory sufficient to justify Japanese support for U.S. operations? To the dismay of the United States, the cold war model offered no clear answer, and Tokyo oscillated (Oberdorfer 1997, 318–320).

Had there actually been a confrontation with North Korea in 1994, the operational impact of Japan's inability to act would have been serious—and the political impact a disaster for the future of the alliance and relations between Tokyo and Washington.

Thus, although many in the Clinton administration wanted to announce the reaffirmation of the Japan-U.S. alliance without taking concrete steps, the predominant view in Tokyo and Washington was that the political credibility of the alliance depended on its operational credibility. U.S. military planners hoped that the Japanese government would be able to just authorize military planning for Korean contingencies without any fanfare. However, the Japanese government had no legal authority to do so. Legislation was required and, for that, a political consensus was essential. The precedent for this was clear in that the 1976 NDPO had been followed by the 1978 U.S.-Japan Defense Guidelines. For the same reasons, Tokyo and Washington decided that after the public revision of the NDPO in 1995, it made sense to authorize the revision of the Defense Guidelines.

The revision of the Defense Guidelines was therefore, by necessity, a public and political act. The Japanese government had to demonstrate clearly to its own people and to the region what the limits were to military cooperation with the United States. Those limits were explained throughout the review, which was completed in September 1997:

- The review would take place within the existing framework of the Japanese constitution and the Japan-U.S. alliance.
- The review would be as transparent as possible to the region.
- The review was not aimed at any specific country or scenario.

The specific functional areas of cooperation are spelled out in the 1997 final report, and had to be in a certain order for the Diet to pass an assortment of legislation, which touched on everything from self-defense to transport and immigration. The thrust of the Guidelines covers Japanese rear-area support, including such missions as the provision of logistics and supplies, and access to civilian and military airports, hospitals, and other facilities. In some cases, rear-area support was strictly constrained by the watchdogs of the Japanese constitution in the Cabinet Legal Affairs Bureau. Thus, for example, Japanese fuel can be provided to U.S. navy ships but Japanese bombs cannot be loaded on U.S. fighters because the latter would constitute Japanese involvement in the use of offensive force. For the most part, though, the support sought by the U.S. forces fit within the constitutional lines drawn by the Cabinet Legal Affairs Bureau. The first installment of Guidelines-related legislation was approved by the Diet in May 1999.

CHINA'S RESPONSE

Because the Guidelines process was transparent and political, China was inevitably an actor—though more of a Greek chorus than a principal. By most accounts, Chinese dissatisfaction focused on perceived transgressions of the status quo: the expansion of Japanese military missions (specifically, minesweeping), the geographic expansion of the alliance, and the inclusion of Taiwan (Christensen 1999; Wu 1999). Each deserves some attention.

EXPANSION OF MILITARY MISSIONS

The expansion of military missions for the Japan Self-Defense Forces did occur, but in 1981—not 1997. In 1981, Tokyo agreed to provide for defense of its own sea lanes up to 1,000 nautical miles. This mission was strictly contained within the defensive shield role Japan had accepted. Thus, the Maritime Self-Defense Forces (MSDF) beefed up their fleet of minesweepers, P-3 patrol planes, escort ships, and Aegis destroyers, but not offensive systems such as amphibious landing ships or aircraft carriers, which were the responsibility of the U.S. Navy. The inclusion of minesweeping and maritime patrols in the 1997 Defense Guidelines does not expand that capability or geographic mission, but it does establish a basis for the same military cooperation in the event of a regional situation in Japan's backyard. In a Korean contingency, for example, MSDF minesweepers would patrol the Sea of Japan, whereas U.S. and South Korean naval minesweepers would handle coastal waters on the peninsula. Offensive operations would not be a dimension of Japan's role under the Guidelines.

EXPANDED GEOGRAPHIC SCOPE

The argument that the geographic scope of the alliance has been expanded is not really true either. When the U.S-Japan Security

Treaty was signed in 1960, Article VI provided for the stationing of U.S. forces in Japan for the "security of the Far East." During the Vietnam War, the government told the Diet that its official definition of the Far East excluded Southeast Asia. For its part, the U.S. government has never officially defined the scope of the Far East clause. In the 1980s, the Japanese and U.S. governments increasingly referred to a "global partnership"—a definition of security cooperation that has no limit, though it does not specifically refer to Article VI of the Treaty. The specific Chinese complaint refers to the 1996 Joint Security Declaration, which describes Japan-U.S. security cooperation in the Asia Pacific region. Because the Joint Security Declaration also includes cooperation on multilateral security dialogue, environmental protection, and other areas beyond Article VI of the Treaty, this is not—strictly speaking—an expansion of the U.S.-Japan Security Treaty's geographic scope. In fact, the rhetorical shift from a global partnership almost suggests a geographic contraction.

TAIWAN'S INCLUSION

The Chinese charge that Taiwan is included in the Guidelines is more complicated. The Guidelines review was, in fact, not scenario-specific —as evidenced by the process aiming to define functional areas of cooperation that could be authorized with specific legislation. The Guidelines, in other words, were not war plans. Still, the Guidelines opened the possibility of greater cooperation in the event of regional contingencies and, thus, the question of whether that could some day include Taiwan remains unresolved.

The Chinese side has insisted that Taiwan be explicitly excluded. Responding to pressure on this subject while visiting Beijing, then Liberal Democratic Party (LDP) Secretary General Katō Kōichi stated, without authority in August 1997, that Taiwan was not covered by the Guidelines. This forced his main political rival and the government's chief spokesperson, Kajiyama Seiroku, to clarify that Taiwan could not be excluded from the Guidelines. Subsequent Chinese criticism on this subject has highlighted Kajiyama's "admission" that Taiwan is covered. The fact remains, however, that Japan and the United States cannot clarify this point one way or the other without undermining regional stability. To exclude Taiwan would signal that Japanese and U.S. security would never be directly affected by conflict in the strait—an unrealistic position. To include Taiwan would send a dangerous signal to Taipei that would only serve to increase regional tensions. There is political support in Japan for cooperation in the widely publicized U.S. contingency plans for the defense of South Korea. However, there is little political appetite in Tokyo for getting embroiled in the military dimension of the Taiwan problem. That may explain why Beijing asks for clarification, knowing fully that there will be none.

Conclusion:
Achieving Enhanced Defense and Security

How then, can China, Japan, and the United States satisfy each other that with regard to the Japan-U.S. Defense Guidelines, no party seeks a significant change in the status quo? Japan and the United States are unlikely to retract any mission already included in the Defense Guidelines. However, Tokyo and Washington should clearly reiterate that the division of roles and missions between the two allies will not change. The decision about whether to revise the Japanese constitution is an internal Japanese affair (polls show that about half of the Japanese population favor doing so). However, the roles and missions of Japan's Self-Defense Forces are a legitimate topic for international dialogue. As the discussion on constitutional revision and the related issue of collective defense proceeds, the Japanese government should lay down clear parameters. Several years ago, former Prime Minister Miyazawa suggested one possible formula in an interview in the *Asahi Shimbun*: Japan will defend itself and provide any support necessary within Japanese territory, but Japan will never use force against a third country. As for Taiwan, Japan and the United States cannot stray from strategic ambiguity and tactical clarity, but they can tell Taipei clearly that the Defense Guidelines are not designed for the defense of Taiwan and have no bearing on either Tokyo's or Washington's "one China" policy. At the same time, Beijing must interpret the ambiguity over the Guidelines' applicability to the Taiwan situation as a clear signal that unprovoked use of force in the Taiwan Strait could well be seen as a legitimate cause for Japan-U.S. defense cooperation.

These confidence-building and transparency measures will go a significant way toward reducing any uncertainties created by the re-affirmation of the Japan-U.S. alliance after the cold war. Ultimately, however, the role of the Japan-U.S. alliance in the trilateral relationship will be determined by larger trends in economic relations, and particularly China's efforts to become an open and competitive player in the global economy. Moreover, the nature of cross-strait dialogue will also set the context for how the Defense Guidelines and the Japan-U.S. alliance will be viewed in Beijing. These two areas—economic cooperation and cross-strait dialogue—are the keys to assuring longer-term security and stability in the trilateral China-Japan-U.S. relationship.

BIBLIOGRAPHY

Christensen, Thomas J. 1999. "China, the U.S.-Japan Alliance, and the Security Dilemma in East Asia." *International Security* 23(4): 49–80.

Cronin, Patrick M., and Michael J. Green. 1994. *Redefining the U.S.-Japan Alliance, Fort McNair Paper 31*. Washington, D.C.: Institute for National Strategic Studies.

Farwell, Byron. 1999. *Over There: The United States in the Great War, 1917–1918*. New York: W. H. Norton.

Ferguson, Niall. 1999. *The Pity of War*. London: Basic Books.

Funabashi Yōichi. 1999. *Alliance Adrift*. New York: Council on Foreign Relations.

Giarra, Paul. 1997. "U.S.-Japan Defense Guidelines: Toward a New Accommodation of Mutual Responsibility." Working paper for "America's Alliance with Japan and Korea in a Changing Northeast Asia." Stanford, Calif.: Asia/Pacific Research Center, Stanford University.

Keegan, John. 1999. *The First World War*. New York: Alfred A. Knopf.

Oberdorfer, Don. 1997. *The Two Koreas: A Contemporary History*. Reading, Mass.: Addison Wesley.

Uriu, Robert. 2000. "The Impact of Policy Ideas: Revisionism and the Clinton Administration's Trade Policy toward Japan." In Gerald Curtis, ed. *New Perspectives on U.S.-Japan Relations*. Tokyo: Japan Center for International Exchange.

Williams, Dan, and Clay Chandler. 1994. "U.S. Aide Sees Relations with Asia in Peril." *Washington Post.* 5 May.
Wu Xinbo. 1999. "Integration on the Basis of Strength: China's Impact on East Asian Security." Working paper for "America's Alliance with Japan and Korea in a Changing Northeast Asia." Stanford, Calif.: Asia/Pacific Research Center, Stanford University.

IV ⚓ China-Japan-U.S. Economic Relations at a Crossroads

Daniel H. Rosen

I N OCTOBER 1999, the ongoing Trilateral Group of younger policy analysts from China, Japan, and the United States gathered in Chiba, Japan, to continue annual discussions in the areas of security, political, and economic relations among their three respective countries. Each country had one representative from each subject area, which provided for an interdisciplinary, comprehensive assessment of three-way relations.

On the economic front, there are three critical questions for the trilateral group of countries to address: (1) whether fundamental economic relations were altered by the receding Asian financial crisis of 1997–1999, (2) whether evolving political and security dimensions will undermine or otherwise alter the economic relationships among the three, and (3) what forces in the economic domain are most likely to affect the security and political domains of the triangle. This chapter will briefly examine these three key questions.

There is one bright spot in economic cooperation that should be mentioned briefly here—the recent passage in the U.S. Senate of permanent normal trade relations (PNTR), previously known as most-favored nation (MFN) status, in exchange for Chinese accession to the World Trade Organization (WTO). This has been the most significant event affecting the three nations' economic relationship in a decade and was a battle hard won in the U.S. House (which passed

This chapter offers views on economic issues of the trilateral relationship from an American, nongovernmental perspective, drawing as it does on my past year in the private sector, and previous years at a nonpartisan, nonprofit Washington, D.C., think tank. Although it is this "think-tank hat" that I here wear, it is a view informed by a strong sense of the critical concerns facing policymakers in the months and years ahead.

the bill in the spring of 2000) and the U.S. Senate (September 2000). Amid the political and security squabbling over Taiwan and the Koreas, the passage of this important economic legislation ensures at least the status quo for some years.

LEGACY OF THE ASIAN FINANCIAL CRISIS

The financial crisis that commenced in Thailand and spread across Asia starting in May 1997 had clear effects on the political, security, and economic status quo throughout the region. Politically, it precipitated regime changes in several developing countries, weakened the legitimacy of governing regimes in several more advanced markets, and altered the consensus about the architecture of the international financial system and the global organization that helps manage it (especially the World Bank and the International Monetary Fund). In terms of security issues, civil unrest came out of the crisis, most violently in the case of Indonesia, leading to the deployment of international peacekeeping forces. Budgetary pressures related to the crisis have had significant effects on military spending in countries across the region, creating a vacuum that less affected countries could choose to fill. The economic effects of the crisis were manifest: Trade patterns shifted markedly away from intraregional trade toward greater dependence on exports to developed markets, especially the U.S. market, and levels of foreign direct investment fell precipitously in several key markets, particularly China.

In the midst of the crisis, a shift in postures among the trilateral countries was evident, although the question remained whether this was tactical and short term or more profound and enduring. This was visible at the November 1998 Trilateral Group meetings at the U.S. Institute for Peace (USIP) in Washington and consisted of a new closeness between Chinese and U.S. analysts who were united in a common cause to battle tentative Japanese policy responses to the regional crisis. At the time, China was committed to a policy of exchange rate stability, despite domestic mercantile pressures to devalue. And although it was clearly a self-interested position, given the ensuing regional economic deterioration that would have come with the collapse of the renminbi, the policy nonetheless lent some stability to the situation and elicited praise from Washington.

In contrast, Japan's great contribution to stemming the crisis should have taken the form of proportionate fiscal stimulus, which never unambiguously occurred, and structural adjustment in the domestic market, which has yet to be implemented. Thus, erstwhile adversaries across the intellectual property rights and market access negotiating tables (China and the United States) suddenly found themselves posturing together against Japanese dawdling.

Another effect of the crisis was to lower the costs to China from a harder line in its rhetoric with Japan. Prior to the crisis, Japan was—and remains—a critical trading partner for China (taking a large share of Chinese exports). Furthermore, Japan is also an important source of direct investment in China, even if it is known to be less forthcoming than other countries with technology transfers due to latent fears of a hollowing out of its manufacturing sector. Nonetheless, the crisis effectively carved away a significant portion of the Sino-Japanese trade that was most elastic, meaning it could be replaced with substitute Japanese production or other foreign production, or done with tolerable adjustment costs. (The preceding effect is typically a market response, not a concerted central action.) With this damage done, the political risk figured in for trade with China by Japan (due to more bellicose rhetoric and cooler bilateral relations) was reduced. Predictably, the willingness of China and Japan to be more confrontational with each other grew for this and other reasons.

Conversely, the importance of the U.S. market—the so-called importer of last resort—rose. In this light, this newly strengthened interdependence in Sino-U.S. trade relations kept the sour bilateral relations of 1997–2000 from becoming even worse. Indeed, the mitigating effect of mutual economic dependence is usually ignored, irresponsibly, by China hawks in the United States precisely because they refuse to admit to the obvious interest of the Chinese in a stable relationship, not strategic competition, to support their absolutely critical export sector. Those exporters are the mainstay of the tax base in China and possess the lion's share of political influence.

The U.S. frustration with weak Japanese responses to the crisis evident at the USIP meeting in 1998 was not superficial. Even sudden Chinese indignation over Japanese fiscal policy management was somewhat opportunistic. The U.S. concern had been building since 1992. The midpoint of the crisis in 1998 was also a turning point for Clinton-era economic policymakers in thinking about the ability of Japan to adapt to seminal changes taking place in the global economy. Thereafter, the number of optimists who advocated working with Japan as a strategic partner for rebuilding the Asian economy on more sustainable market foundations were fewer. Indeed, in 2000 Japan had gone back into recession, while talk of the shape of a "new Japan" continued at home. This was the same quarter that the South Korean economy, which adjusted less haltingly, grew at a year-on-year rate of 13 percent.

Therefore, it appears that the fundamental basis of economic relations among the three nations has been altered, with the financial crisis hastening these changes rather than causing them per se. Other contributing factors at this post–cold war point in history include the marketization of the Chinese economy and Japan's inability to effect a transition from successful central planning (in an era when assiduous coordination in a homogeneous country with strategic home market protection tolerated by trading partners was possible) to a strategy more responsive to global technology, supply, and demand trends. Japan is expected to be limping for too long to be of any strategic importance in shaping the economic institutional questions currently brewing in Asia, questions that must include South Asia— particularly India.

In part due to the financial crisis, China today is more uncertain about its development strategy than it was three years ago when the Japan/South Korea–inspired "grab the big, release the small" plan to craft one hundred Chinese *keiretsu* provided a clear plan. Therefore, China is not interested in filling the role of Japanese economic missionary in the region, preoccupied as it is with gargantuan economic challenges at home for which it does not yet have answers. This leaves the United States more in a vacuum of ideas than ever, still enjoying (conveniently) the most robust economic expansion in the world. And yet, Japanese and Chinese economic insecurities, different as they are, share a common interest in not permitting a triumphant United States from proselytizing in their backyards. Alas, though, the Silicon Valley private sector is already doing that decisively.

IMPACT OF POLITICS AND SECURITY
ON THE ECONOMIC REALM

The economic relationship among China, Japan, and the United States is mutually enriching, despite the endless trade disputes and trilateral wrangling. Such wrangling is normal. As undisputed as the logic of free commerce among nations now is (thanks to more than one hundred years of competition between market and nonmarket systems), it does not take place in a vacuum. Political and security considerations have a major influence on the ability of societies to specialize along comparative advantage and exchange goods/services lines. Here we address what influence political and security considerations have on trilateral economic relations in the period ahead, and whether they will undermine economic development.

To explore these questions, let us identify some political/security situations in the region that affect all three parties, and then consider their impact on the three economies. We will focus on the cases of cross-strait relations and Korean peninsula stability, which form the cross-beams to the China-Japan-U.S. axis and are most relevant in this regard. Both cases involve security threats intertwined with political dynamics and large-scale economic relationships, and, in addition to involving all three countries, they will likely simmer for a considerable time yet.

Tensions in the Taiwan and Korean cases have the potential to affect the economic development of China, Japan, and the United States by (1) interrupting trade flows, (2) amplifying financial market volatility, (3) depressing investment flows, and (4) delaying the formation of or action in international economic management regimes. Regional trade flows are already significantly distorted by China-Taiwan tensions, as cross-strait trade is largely intermediated through Hong Kong or Japan (never mind for the moment that a large volume has been smuggled into China directly through coastal ports such as Xiamen, a practice some senior officials are trying to eliminate). In the case of China-U.S. economic relations, this intermediation has further muddied efforts to clarify the origin of goods for quota purposes.

In the future, Taiwanese President Chen Shui-bian's pledge to remove some direct trade restrictions, as well as the impending significant fall in tariffs associated with Chinese and Taiwanese WTO accession, should dramatically increase the volume of trade among China, Taiwan, Japan, and the United States. (China-Taiwan direct trade should amount to perhaps $30 billion–$40 billion following WTO normalization.) However, supply uncertainties due to the political and security tensions in the Taiwan Strait would greatly distort these flows by increasing the transaction costs (i.e., insurance) of trade flows exposed to political risk. Similar risk premiums are, of course, attached to trade in the Korean sphere.

With time, however, expectations about future instabilities are based more on deeds than words and, in this sense, the powers in the region have been more conservative in action than rhetoric. In fact, the risk premium reflected in trade flows in North Asia seems to have come down to the point where underlying competitiveness is more important than political risk in determining trade. Thus, shy of a dramatic escalation of tensions, the present extent of occasional political and security flare-ups in the region does not appear likely to radically sway the China-Japan-U.S. dynamic in terms of trade flows.

Financial market stability is a different story. Money is fungible and even more mobile than traded goods, and it is more dependent on long-term institutional stability. Consequently, the Taiwanese and Korean political tensions and security questions do have the potential to inflict real damage on the China-Japan-U.S. economic relationship over time.

It is natural that developed countries' (Japan and the United States) savings flow from their mature markets to China's higher-growth emerging market in the present period. However, Chinese missiles in the vicinity of Taiwan and North Korean missiles over Japan have major impacts on financial market volatility, undermining the normal investment of capital in overseas countries. There are long institutional memories in these markets, and with near perfect capital mobility a long-term incentive is created to move funds to safe-haven markets, such as New York. This scenario precludes an efficient diversification of investment over the range of opportunities in the trilateral economies and prevents the mitigating effect of cross-holding on policy rhetoric and military adventurism. In short, even the present level of political and security tension in the region will disrupt the formation of optimal, healthy, and stable financial markets over the long run, and that is not in the interest of China, Japan, or the United States.

The same holds true for cross-border investment. Though high levels of direct investment in China (much from Japan and the United States, but the most from Taiwan—the very party with which China has the most rancorous security relationship) were sustained through the tensions of the 1990s, it is not a foregone conclusion that such investment levels will continue. These heavy volumes may have been anomalous, as foreign investors sought to make up for the abnormally low Chinese baseline of investment and relatively permissive investment rules post-1992. But the considerable investment downturn since 1998 suggests the heavy volume was not the long-term level. In the future, lower annual flows from Japan and the United States may be more sensitive to political and security tensions because hard-core investors have already gone in, and because investors were burned by the economic downturn of recent years and, hence, may be more cautious.

Political and security tensions in 2000–2002 will probably not knock status quo economic relations among the trilateral countries off track or alter linear growth significantly once China's WTO accession is completed. The main reason for this relatively stable outlook is that in each country the central focus of these years will be domestic restructuring. In China and Japan, this involves structural adjustment across the spectrum of industrial sectors, including major opening to import competition. In the United States, there is a different kind of restructuring afoot—restructuring domestic political consensus in favor of global economic engagement. Mostly due to the sales pitches of politicians and special interest groups who are stirring up discontent to attract support, there are now broad (though superficial) divisions in American society about the nature and advisability of globalization. If the next U.S. president cannot quickly turn this around, the United States will be disengaged from shaping Asia Pacific economic regimes for some time to come.

With all three of these key Asia Pacific economies bogged down with domestic considerations, each will be eager to maintain the status quo: the present slate of political dynamics and security issues and, in turn, an economic scene no more aggravated by the former factors than it already is.

This brings us to the fourth economic area where politics and security matters have the ability to disrupt trilateral economic affairs—international regime building. If the present economic interaction among these three countries simply continues growing at the present rate, the institutional structures needed to gird that growth will need to be improved. When financial flows boomed without institutional growth in the mid-1990s, a financial crisis resulted, due in large part to insufficient oversight and regulation. If trade and investment growth return to pre–Asian crisis levels, this need becomes even more urgent (indeed, several regional economies, such as South Korea, once again have blistering growth well above 10 percent). China's WTO accession provides one such institutional structure for managing trade disputes among the three, but more complicated trade-related issues are not covered adequately in the WTO (e.g., competition policy).

Progress in building the institutional structures needed to manage Asian economic growth during this period of immense transition cannot be attained with the status quo, unlike the case with trade or investment flows. Each political or security altercation involving the trilateral group has the serious potential to put off work on pending institutional business, as the Yugoslavia embassy bombing did to stall WTO accession negotiations in the summer of 1999. A number of regime-building exercises have barely been identified, let alone are pending, and even fewer are likely to be pursued when security disagreements lead to broken economic dialogues. Therefore, security and political problems have the serious potential to interfere with economic regime-building activities. Thus, this is perhaps the most important area of concern in the China-Japan-U.S. economic relationship in the medium term. If these regimes are not crafted in the medium term, the long-term growth rates in Asia will be assuredly less than optimal.

IMPACT OF ECONOMICS ON POLITICS AND SECURITY

Conversely, the economic leg of the trilateral relationship has demonstrable effects on the political and security cones. In fact, the increasing relative importance of trade with the U.S. market to Asia may have tempered Chinese actions toward the United States. (Yes, relations would have been even worse without hundreds of billions of dollars in Chinese trade surpluses in recent years.) On the other hand, the diminution of China-Japan trade at the midpoint of the financial crisis probably augmented the bellicosity of Chinese postures toward Japan over the proximate causes of Taiwan and the Japan-U.S. Defense Guidelines revisions.

More fundamentally, the impact of economic development on the political mix among the three comes in the form of the connection between income growth and political liberalization. That there is even a causal relationship here is hotly debated. Nonetheless, the correlation is strong, the anecdotal evidence as to why this would be the case is sound, and Chinese intellectuals confirm that the regime is already keying political reforms against benchmark levels of per capita gross national product (GNP) for purposes of long-term transition planning.

Protecting economic activity is also a core purpose of political and security activities. In the case of Japan and the United States, economic extension beyond their home borders is already global. The change at the margin is coming from China. Chinese interests will extend further afield than ever before, as China evolves from a regional economic player to one that has tentacles extending worldwide. Energy security, in particular, will draw Chinese force projection out of its traditional radius, as this is the key area of Chinese strategic vulnerability. Nonetheless, primary Chinese vulnerabilities—and hence motivations—are in fact domestic, in the form of structural transitions, despite recent attempts to fit China into the box of "strategic competitor."

CONCLUSION

The effects of the Asian financial crisis and its aftermath have contributed to altered fundamentals in three-way economic relations among China, Japan, and the United States. However, the changes taking place have to do with the unfolding forces of globalization that go beyond the capital flow intermediation problems at the core of the financial crisis of 1997–1999. Importantly, these changes include technological innovations that are redistributing comparative advantage and related institutional shifts involved in making this technology diffusion meaningful and lasting. The most notable trilateral change has been a less compelling economic role for Japan, both in driving regional economic growth through imports and foreign investment, and in providing a dominant growth strategy model for the region. Another key shift is the rate of economic and civil liberalization in China that has greatly expanded its economic influence.

Finally, I have argued that in terms of the interplay among economics, politics, and security in the three-way relationship, the predominant impulse is for the status quo. Economic development is the linchpin for success in all three realms in all three countries, and the critical challenges facing each country have to do with domestic adjustment. Nonetheless, the longer-term basis of the trilateral relationship requires substantial regime building to help nurture and maintain economic growth, and this is a task made difficult by the present tendency for political and security friction to delay proactive cooperation to strengthen regimes.

The completion of China's WTO accession process should produce a boom in confidence about cooperation and lend momentum to efforts to put in place further structures to manage commerce. If all three countries succeed in meeting their respective domestic challenges—structural adjustment and financial reform in China, import liberalization and fiscal stimulus in Japan, and rebuilt political consensus in favor of international economic engagement in the United States—then after 2002 we should see a renaissance in constructive activity among the three to secure the benefits of hard-won marketization efforts in East Asia.

V ⚘ Korea's Influence on Northeast Asian Major Power Relations

Scott Snyder

THE GEOGRAPHY OF NORTHEAST ASIA, where three major powers physically meet and their interests intersect, has placed the Korean peninsula in a position of dubious privilege. Surrounded by larger and more powerful neighbors, Korea has been the bridge over which significant cultural influences have passed and the point at which conflicting interests have intersected—a battleground on which major powers sought primacy from the end of the nineteenth and throughout the twentieth century. Korea continues to stand at the crossroads of Northeast Asia's major power relationships; the division of the peninsula itself is a testament to the continuing centrality of the Korean peninsula as a reflection of past power struggles and as a likely venue for the reshaping of Northeast Asia's regional security relationships in the decades to come. Unlike the end of the nineteenth century, when a declining, emasculated, dynastic Korea could exert little influence on regional rivalries, at the dawn of the twenty-first century, a rapidly industrializing, democratic South Korea has emerged as a significant middle power, with potential influence as a mediator—or perhaps instigator—of regional rivalries.

If events on the Korean peninsula are likely to be a driving force in shaping a new Northeast Asian security environment, do recent events on the peninsula predicate a positive or negative trend for major power relations in the region, particularly among China, Japan, and the United States? In what ways is the gradual, yet significant, shift in the balance of power on the Korean peninsula (between North and South Korea) during the past decade influencing relations among these three regional powers, and what challenges will this shift pose for regional stability? Will an emerging South Korea have an influence on the major power relationships in Asia that is neutral or decisive? Confrontational or peaceful? And, finally, what of North Korea's role—is the North's influence declining or actually driving the tenuous regional security agenda and, thus, shaping the regional security balance (as in 1998 and 1999)?

Ironically, the first priority in the respective capitals of the major regional powers is the focus on each other, and Korea-related affairs are generally secondary considerations. Yet Korea constitutes the reality that tests policy concepts, lays bare true intentions, and inhibits the complete transition to truly post–cold war relationships among China, Japan, and the United States. Can the major powers themselves manage a strategy that takes into account their broader interests, while simultaneously managing issues on the Korean peninsula that may derail the agenda?

To shed light on these questions, I will examine the following issues: (1) the impact of North Korea's decline and unconventional nuclear and missile threats on the security strategies of China, Japan, the United States, and Russia during the past decade; (2) South Korean President Kim Dae Jung's diplomacy toward the major powers; and (3) the ramifications of recent trends in missile proliferation and theater missile defense (TMD) on regional security relations. Then I will proceed to draw preliminary conclusions about possible influences Korean peninsula developments may have on the trilateral (China-Japan-U.S.) relationship.

IMPACT OF NORTH KOREA'S DECLINE ON REGIONAL SECURITY RELATIONS

North Korea's failure to take advantage of external economic and political factors that determine national power has led to an increasingly decisive shift in the 1990s in favor of South Korea. The seeds of North Korea's own failure are its inability to develop an effective strategy for fostering economic growth due to its highly centralized, self-reliant, and autarkic industrial model—a process that was accelerated by North Korea's inability to pursue reforms in response to changing economic and political circumstances. The collapse of the Soviet Union and subsequent loss of economic and political support from its major allies sent North Korea into a downward spiral of economic decline that has accelerated South Korea's economic and political dominance. The shift itself—albeit gradual and incomplete —and North Korea's response to its own decline have shaped the regional security agenda and the priorities of the major powers as they have responded to perceived instability and sought to restore the status quo ante.

As a driving force for shaping the hierarchy of regional security concerns of the major powers, North Korea's tactical responses to its own precarious situation have defined the security agenda in Northeast Asia in the following ways: (1) the nature of North Korea's initial post–cold war challenge placed the issue of nuclear proliferation at the top of the Asian security agenda (Mazarr 1995); (2) the prospect of either North Korea's political collapse or the renewed outbreak of military conflict between the two Koreas highlighted the unsustainability of the internal Korean peninsula status quo while inducing regional neighbors to act to prevent destabilization on the peninsula; (3) North Korea became a shared security concern, thus providing a concrete focus for enhanced multilateral consultation and coordination among regional powers; and (4) the perpetuation of a divided Korea (i.e., North Korea's continued quest for regime survival) has, thus far, prevented the emergence of new and potentially divisive regional security dilemmas.

North Korea's four "contributions" to Northeast Asia's regional security agenda have somewhat contradictorily affected the regional relationships among China, Japan, and the United States, with South Korean choices also playing a major role. The well-documented events that have accompanied North Korea's nuclear threat, economic decline, and continued pursuit of unconventional means by which to prop up its regime in the 1990s suggest some conclusions about the ways in which North Korea's actions have shaped post–cold war regional security relationships between the trilateral powers (see Oberdorfer 1997; Sigal 1998).

THE NORTH KOREAN NUCLEAR THREAT

The emergence of the North Korean nuclear threat and the initiation of a UN Security Council–endorsed bilateral North Korean-U.S. negotiation channel, which led to the North Korean-U.S. Geneva Agreed

Framework, has deepened American involvement on the Korean peninsula and given the United States a larger stake in the successful management of a peaceful process of tension reduction between the two Koreas. Strong South Korean-U.S. bilateral coordination will remain a critical factor in determining the extent of U.S. effectiveness, even while the United States engages in a new relationship with North Korea. Increased U.S. involvement in Korean affairs carries with it the advantages of influence but also the responsibilities and dangers of leadership. If not effectively managed in the context of the broader regional security balance, U.S. efforts might damage U.S. influence and interests in the region. The United States must work to ensure that it is perceived as neither irrelevant nor obstructionist in the process of inter-Korean tension reduction and eventual reunification.

DESTABILIZING EFFECTS OF
NORTH KOREAN WEAKNESS ON ASIA

Concerns among regional neighbors about the potential ramifications of refugee flows and other destabilizing effects of North Korea's provocative political behavior and weakness have driven China and the United States together in maintaining stability on the Korean peninsula (Snyder 1996). This is best epitomized in a shared Sino-U.S. "three no's" policy toward the Korean peninsula that has underscored gradually increasing bilateral cooperation vis-à-vis North Korea: "No nukes, no war, and no collapse of North Korea." China prefers not to see a U.S.-dominated Korean peninsula in the long term, but in the short term there are shared interests in maintaining regional stability in an area adjoining China. In many respects, the conundrum of just how to coax North Korea into cooperation to ensure regional stability is shared by Chinese and American policymakers, despite their divergent respective positions as a "friend" and an "enemy" of North Korea.

IMPLEMENTATION OF THE GENEVA AGREED FRAMEWORK

The establishment of a formalized mechanism for implementing the Geneva Agreed Framework through the Korean Peninsula Energy Development Organization (KEDO) represents an initial, yet incomplete, step toward enhanced multilateral security cooperation that has developed in direct response to North Korea's nuclear threat. In 1993–1994, this political coordination process among Japan, the United States, and South Korea (including consultations with China) originally focused on the consideration of economic sanctions designed to punish North Korea's alleged nuclear weapons development efforts. KEDO has laid the foundation for increased formalized cooperation among the aforementioned countries. This cooperation has included the provision of support for increased trilateral coordination in the areas of contingency planning to respond to the possibility of a North Korean collapse; the establishment of the Trilateral Coordination and Oversight Group of senior-level officials from Japan, the United States, and South Korea in April 1999; and an unprecedented trilateral summit meeting between Prime Minister Obuchi Keizō, President Bill Clinton, and President Kim Dae Jung on the sidelines of the Asia-Pacific Economic Cooperation (APEC) forum meeting in New Zealand in September 1999.

These steps toward increased policy coordination in response to North Korean nuclear and missile proliferation threats have facilitated a level of institutionalized cooperation between Japan, the United States, and South Korea that regionalizes U.S.-led alliance coordination in Northeast Asia in the absence of more active participation by China and Russia. All the countries in the region (including China, which is not a KEDO member) have an interest in ensuring that the Korean peninsula remains nonnuclear, and KEDO has become the primary vehicle for pursuing that objective. The question of whether China and Russia find themselves cooperating with or confronting the Japan-South Korean-U.S. cooperation process institutionalized by former U.S. Defense Secretary William Perry could be one possible indicator of the extent to which broader regional cooperation may be institutionalized in the future (Snyder 1999).

FAILURE TO
ESTABLISH NORTHEAST ASIA SUBREGIONAL DIALOGUE

Although North Korea's perceived provocations have driven enhanced security cooperation and consultations (particularly among Japan, South Korea, and the United States, and KEDO), it has not yet proven feasible to establish a subregional dialogue mechanism in Northeast Asia, largely due to North Korean refusals to participate in such a forum. Meanwhile, the Northeast Asia Cooperation Dialogue project has established regular track-two discussions among China, Japan, South Korea, Russia, and the United States. Furthermore, calls for a formal six-party dialogue have increased in frequency, with separate proposals from Japanese Prime Minister Obuchi and South Korean Prime Minister Kim Jong P'il in 1998. Among the critical issues are the need to distinguish between the role of a subregional security dialogue and the purposes of the Four-Party Talks among the two Koreas, China, and the United States to bring a formal end to the Korean War. At the same time, a regional agenda for managing missile proliferation and responding to environmental and maritime issues, quite apart from the Korean questions addressed through the Four-Party framework, is becoming a matter of increasing urgency that may necessarily lead to an expansion of multilateral dialogue and cooperation.

Prospects for regional economic cooperation remain limited by political tensions and by lack of infrastructure and the failure of the North Korean political leadership to grasp the importance of systemic reforms as a vehicle for enhancing economic growth. Although the UN-sponsored Tumen River Area Development Project of the early 1990s was an ambitious attempt to stimulate trade and investment relationships across regional boundaries where North Korea, China, and Russia meet, the project has proved to be overly ambitious and premature. Additional U.S. steps toward the lifting of economic sanctions constitute an important symbolic step toward easing political tensions and helping remove a long-standing North Korean excuse for its own poor economic performance. To the extent that the lifting of U.S. economic sanctions can help North Korean leaders recognize the limitations of their own structure, such lifting may be a prerequisite for the promotion of necessary adjustments inside North Korea and as a first step toward integration of the North Korean economy with that of the outside world. However, regional economic growth between North Korea, China, and Russia will only flourish with the removal of the old cold war boundaries and the promotion of greater cross-border contacts—for example, the limited progress made in establishing local farmers' markets in North Korea as a result of the opening that accompanied the 1996–1997 food crisis.

SOUTH KOREA'S RELATIONS WITH MAJOR POWERS UNDER KIM DAE JUNG

PROMOTING COOPERATION AND REGIONAL BALANCE

A relatively new characteristic of the regional security dynamic in Northeast Asia in the late 1990s was the balanced and effective diplomacy of South Korea under President Kim Dae Jung. President Kim has pursued a steady and well-developed set of priorities in his foreign relations with major powers. The implementation of this approach has clearly set forth South Korean diplomatic objectives and priorities, has sought support from and emphasized coordination with South Korea's larger neighbors over its North Korean policy objectives, and has demonstrated a deep understanding of South Korea's regional environment, including the potential balancing role South Korea can play in lessening regional tensions while at the same time pursuing South Korean strategic interests. Kim Dae Jung's consistency is particularly striking when compared with the approach of his predecessor, Kim Young Sam, who maintained a rather difficult relationship with the United States and played up regional rivalries —most notably by joining with Chinese President Jiang Zemin in a strident criticism of Japan's historical legacy on Jiang's visit to Seoul in 1995. Although the new Bush administration's harder line toward North Korea has frustrated Kim Dae Jung, the primacy of U.S.-ROK coordination in dealing with North Korea remains evident.

President Kim initiated his major power diplomacy with a June 1998 state visit to Washington. During his meeting with President Clinton, Kim sought support for his policy of engagement with North Korea and was lauded for his lifelong efforts to promote democracy in Korea. Most significantly, the visit symbolized the primacy of the South Korean-U.S. relationship and set the tone for a close consultative bilateral relationship in pursuit of shared security interests. Although subsequent suspicions regarding whether North Korea was secretly developing a nuclear reprocessing site at Keumchang-ri and the August 1998 Taep'odong launch threatened to open a gap between Kim's focus on engagement and a possibly harder-line U.S. policy approach toward North Korea, the Kim administration adapted itself to reflect U.S. concerns about North Korea's missile development and export program while continuing to insist on a coordinated engagement policy (Sanger 1998; see also "A List of Japanese Companies" 1999). In the end, President Kim's patient and persistent efforts were sufficient to convince former U.S. Defense Secretary William Perry to pursue engagement of North Korea (on the condition that North Korea froze its missile testing program). Secretary Perry's advocacy of a comprehensive approach to North Korea may be regarded as a victory for President Kim's joint approach to policy coordination with the United States, a process that has removed much of the disharmony and ill feeling that had dominated South Korean-U.S. consultations under former President Kim Young Sam.

Even more impressive was Kim Dae Jung's subsequent ability to remove (at least temporarily) the stumbling block of history from the Japan-South Korean relationship during his October 1998 visit to Tokyo to meet Prime Minister Obuchi. During that visit, Kim emphasized reconciliation and went out of his way to praise the contributions of Japan's dynamic economic growth to Asian prosperity rather than harping on Japan's past misdeeds and colonization of Korea. In return, Kim received a written statement of regret for Japan's history of oppression against Korea, and a basis for broader Japan-South Korean economic and security cooperation was thus forged. The backdrop for this significant progress was the effect of the Asian financial crisis on the Japanese and Korean economies, and the psychological impact of the North Korean Taep'odong launch that flew over Japan six weeks prior to Kim's visit to Tokyo. Although mutual suspicions remain under the surface, the rapid development of the Japan-South Korean security relationship to include regular military-to-military exchanges, joint exercises, and contingency planning in response to possible North Korean instability are the most significant fruits of the improved relationship. Perhaps the most dramatic measure of the extent to which President Kim's diplomacy toward Japan has been successful, however, was the failure of China's President Jiang to receive a similar written apology from Prime

Minister Obuchi during his visit to Tokyo the following month—an act that precipitated serious public criticism of Japan by President Jiang and exposed the deep distrust that stands in the way of a satisfactory Sino-Japanese relationship.

President Kim has consistently acknowledged China's interests in stability on the Korean peninsula, and Kim's emphasis on a gradual process of reconciliation between North and South rather than on short-term Korean reunification is no doubt a welcome statement for a Chinese leadership that so prizes stability on the Korean peninsula. China has been increasingly willing to support South Korean interests rather than supporting North Korea for the sake of enhancing stability on the Korean peninsula. President Kim's visit to China in November 1998 quietly opened the door to expanded Sino-South Korean relations heretofore boosted primarily by a burgeoning economic relationship that had reached $28 billion per year in trade by the end of 2000. The Kim Dae Jung administration has quietly secured key political and security concessions from China that had previously not been available out of consideration for the historical relationship between Beijing and Pyongyang. Most notable in this regard have been the initiation of defense minister–level military dialogues and the opening of a South Korean consulate in Shenyang (Liaoning province) after more than seven years of negotiations. After a bilateral consultation in Auckland, New Zealand, in conjunction with the APEC meeting in September 1999, President Kim went out of his way to give credit to counterpart Jiang Zemin for playing a significant role in convincing North Korea to defer plans of further long-range missile testing.

Some critics might argue that, in fact, the Kim Dae Jung administration has been overly accommodating to China following South Korean Defense Minister Cho Song-tae's August 1999 visit to Beijing. Cho raised some eyebrows in a lecture at China's National Defense University when he stated that the disposition of U.S. forces following Korean unification "shall be decided by unanimous agreement among Northeastern Asian countries." This controversial statement stimulated enough opposition in South Korea's National Assembly to call for Cho's resignation, and the statement represents a remarkable departure from past assurances by President Kim that the presence of U.S. forces in Korea would be a force for regional stability even after Korean unification. Although Cho's remarks were publicly contested by critics who are strongly supportive of a continued long-term South Korean-U.S. security relationship, Cho was not forced to resign over his remarks, and South Korea is reticent to join the Japan-U.S. TMD project. This suggests that the debate among South Korean security analysts has broadened in recent years beyond the focus on the United States in careful consideration of Chinese interests and potential influence on the Korean peninsula. This development must give Beijing some encouragement concerning the prospects for a deepened long-term relationship with South Korea.

The final stage of Kim Dae Jung's focus on major powers came in May 1999 in his Moscow summit with ailing President Boris Yeltsin. President Kim won support from Yeltsin for his "Sunshine Policy" of engagement with North Korea, and Russia agreed to continue to supply South Korea with a variety of Russian military equipment as barter payment for the $3 billion in aid and credits given to Russia by President Roh Tae Woo after normalization with the Soviet Union a decade earlier. With the establishment of cooperative and supportive relationships between South Korea and the major powers, Kim has shown a remarkable degree of leadership and initiative and has stored up political capital in his attempts to gain regional support for his engagement policies with North Korea.

Most notable among Kim's diplomatic achievements, however, is that South Korea's gain comes not from pitting larger adversaries against each other (a traditional Korean approach to preserving space against possibly threatening interests of larger neighbors most effectively used by Pyongyang), but rather by indirectly stimulating cooperation in pursuit of common regional interests. Kim has emphasized the important long-term stabilizing role of the U.S. military presence in the Asia Pacific region even more effectively than former U.S. Secretary of Defense William Cohen, whose own assertions to that effect were much less well-received than Kim's endorsement of a long-term balancing role for the U.S. military in Asia. In addition, South Korea has been a leading proponent of subregional dialogue in Northeast Asia to further deepen cooperative security interests and to dampen possibilities for major power confrontation ("Seoul Muses" 1999). At the same time, the limits of a positive South Korean diplomatic influence on major power relations have also become apparent: as was seen in 1998 and 1999, South Korea can do little to prevent downturns in either the Sino-Japanese relationship or Sino-U.S. relations.

NORTH KOREAN MISSILE TESTING AND THE TMD DEBATE

North Korea's missile development efforts—highlighted by the August 31, 1998, launch of a three-stage Taep'odong missile with capabilities greater than those anticipated by the intelligence community —have served as a catalyst for an increased focus on missile proliferation and missile defense efforts as part of the Asia Pacific security equation, an issue that has been a central focus of the China-Japan-U.S. relationship. Perhaps more significant than the North Korean launch itself has been the increased impetus for development of TMD in Japan and the United States, and the strong opposition in Beijing to the possible deployment of such a system.

Several factors affect the dynamics of the TMD debate in Tokyo and Washington. First, much of the political momentum for the project comes from American "can-do" faith in technological capabilities and a desire to meet a challenging technical goal rather than a realistic consideration of the application of TMD to security dynamics in the Asia Pacific region. In addition, domestic politics have played a major role in pushing this project forward, an outgrowth of Ronald Reagan's "Star Wars" project legacy. Finally, the fact that the U.S. intelligence community failed to accurately predict North Korean missile capabilities following the release of the Rumsfeld Report (July 1998), which warned that rogue states were rapidly developing such capabilities, has added momentum to political arguments that a national missile defense (NMD) system is needed. Conceptually, the ideal of an airtight security shield to protect America and its troops and facilities abroad from external threats imposed by challenges to American dominance is appealing, even if 100 percent security is impossible to guarantee.

As a concept that has garnered widespread political support in the United States, the TMD train has already left the station; the key questions now are how large an investment will be needed to develop such a system, over what time frame,[1] and which states may have access to such systems. Nonetheless, the desirability and ramifications of TMD deployment are questions that will require assessments of impact on the region and the wider global system. These questions are just beginning to be entertained in the context of upcoming negotiations with Russia over how and whether the Anti-Ballistic Missile (ABM) Treaty may be amended (Hoffman 1999). Some Asian regional security analysts have expressed concerns that TMD deployment could prematurely or unnecessarily force choices that would lead to a confrontational China-U.S. relationship (Manning and Przystup 1999, 62–65). For the near and mid terms, it is important to keep in mind that (upper-tier) TMD remains a concept, not a field-ready deployable system, or even a completely effective defensive shield.

In the Asia Pacific region, the TMD debate has become a debate over future intentions, a surrogate in Beijing for exploring whether the long-term objectives of Japan and the United States in developing TMD are threatening or purely defensive.[2] By the same token, any complaints in Beijing that TMD may hamper the effectiveness of "missile deterrence," or coercion to prevent the possible declaration of Taiwan's independence, are seen by many in Washington as confirmation of Beijing's aggressive intentions. The initial appeal of TMD deployment is that it turns the conventional cold war concepts of security on their head, replacing the concept of mutual assured destruction with the idea of mutual assured defense.

This concept may be particularly appealing in Japan, which has cultivated a culture and constitutional interpretation that has foresworn offensive military capabilities of its own since World War II. In addition, there are growing concerns in Japan that lack of offense in a post–cold war security environment may make Japan particularly vulnerable to coercion from neighbors with offensive missile capabilities. From this perspective, it is natural that Japan might seek to acquire "the shield without the sword." However, the idea of mutual assured defense versus mutual assured deterrence represents an epistemological change that is unlikely to be easily accepted in Beijing. One Chinese critic of this Japanese perception recently asserted that the decision to develop TMD undermines efforts to establish a regional or international missile control regime, and Japan's position is not purely defensive in the context of the Japan-U.S. military alliance. Rather, in response to TMD, "the PRC [China] must accelerate military research. The PRC must improve its sword."[3] Such comments illustrate that the TMD issue will be viewed in asymmetric terms unless the capacity to deploy defenses against incoming missile launches is indeed mutual.

The TMD and NMD debate in the United States will have larger ramifications beyond technical feasibility and big power reactions. It is by no means clear, for example, that domestic policy or political considerations will produce assessments of what is best for the U.S. national interest. In particular, it is legitimate to question the ability of American domestic politics to take into account the possibility that U.S. actions will harden the views of those in the international community who see U.S. intervention as malevolent. Thus, the idea that Americans can choose between internationalism or isolationism is a false choice; a more constructive debate would be directed to properly take into consideration how to enhance the quality and attractiveness of American actions to a global constituency so as to perpetuate and strengthen U.S. leadership internationally.

LONG-TERM REGIONAL INTERESTS AND THE KOREAN PENINSULA

We have seen that events on the Korean peninsula have played a major, perhaps even decisive, role in shaping security trends in Northeast Asia. The situation on the Korean peninsula affects and is affected by the triangular China-Japan-U.S. relationship as well as the nature and quality of the respective bilateral relationships. The triangular relationships of the respective major powers with Pyongyang and Seoul add a level of complexity to the regional relationships that must be managed carefully to assure regional stability. Specifically, it is worth highlighting the following conclusions.

- It is conventional wisdom that good China-U.S. relations are necessary for positive progress in inter-Korean relations, yet the question of which direction a unified Korea leans diplomatically could engender competition for a close relationship with Seoul. In particular, China will want to maintain a friendly relationship with a unified Korea that shares a common border, and the United States may hope to maintain its troop presence and alliance relationship with a unified Korean ally. A continued U.S. presence in post-reunification Korea may be perceived negatively by China, which has its own version of a Monroe Doctrine for former tributary states and near neighbors. If the conflict of interest engenders premature competition for influence in Korea between China and the United States, many issues of a future unified Korea may be difficult to resolve.

• Japan shares strategic interests with the United States under the Japan-U.S. security alliance, the revitalization of which Chinese leaders have vocally opposed. Even more complicated is the fact that China and Japan have equivalent and potentially conflicting needs to maintain positive relations with the leadership of a re-unified Korea to assure their respective security interests. Given the negative Chinese public attitudes toward the Japanese and the inability of the two countries to settle issues of historical responsibility from World War II, the agenda for Sino-Japanese political cooperation has remained limited. As progress is made in managing inter-Korean tension reduction, special attention should be given to ensuring that Sino-Japanese confrontation or competition does not develop over Korea. One challenge for Korean diplomacy will be to effectively manage its respective relationships with China and Japan.

• The nascent development of regional economic ties between China, Japan, and South Korea could be a mitigating force that lessens the possibility of direct military conflict by stimulating prospects for economic cooperation and mutual prosperity. Economic interdependence between China/Japan and China/South Korea are relatively recent developments that may serve to mitigate the severity of political disputes if the costs of confrontation and the benefits of cooperation are sufficiently high. The Tumen River Area Development Project posits that with the end of inter-Korean confrontation, political tensions will be sufficiently low that Japanese and South Korean capital and technology will join with North Korean and Russian labor and natural resources to drive decades of regional growth, development, and prosperity.

• Korean events such as the inter-Korean summit of June 2000 will clearly stimulate responses that may affect each of the bilateral relationships among the major powers by contributing to the overall context and shaping specific issues that must be dealt with to ensure Northeast Asian stability. Precipitous actions or status quo–challenging developments in North Korea have recently had a negative impact on major power relations through the challenges of nuclear and missile proliferation, and shifts in the Korean diplomatic balance may also influence major power relations negatively if Korean interests are perceived to tilt too much in the direction of one neighbor. In fact, playing larger powers against each other has been a time-honored Korean strategy for survival in an unfriendly neighborhood. Nonetheless, recent trends in South Korean diplomacy suggest the possibility of a more sophisticated and constructive approach, whereby Korean efforts to balance and constructively engage the major powers in areas of common interest—through the development of multilateral dialogue and regional cooperation on nuclear and missile proliferation issues, for example—could become a strong drive for cooperation across former economic, political, and ideological boundaries.

NOTES

1. "Only three flight tests are now scheduled before President Clinton faces a decision next summer over whether to field a national anti-missile system by 2005 at an estimated cost between now and then of $10.5 billion" (Graham 1999, A22).

2. A more detailed treatment of Chinese views of Japan-U.S. cooperation to develop TMD, as well as a sobering description of the alliance adjustments that would be required for TMD to be successfully deployed, appears in Green and Cronin (1999, 170–188, 311–322).

3. This comment was made as part of a discussion at the Council for Security Cooperation in the Asia Pacific (CSCAP) North Pacific Working Group meeting, Tokyo, Japan, September 27–28, 1999.

BIBLIOGRAPHY

Cha, Victor D. 1999. "Engaging China: Seoul-Beijing Détente and Korean Security." *Survival* 41(1): 73–98.

Graham, Bradley. 1999. "Missile Defense Plan Scores a Direct Hit; 'Kill Vehicle' Intercepts, Obliterates Unarmed Minuteman over Central Pacific." *Washington Post* (3 October): A22.

Green, Michael J., and Patrick M. Cronin, eds. 1999. *The U.S.-Japan Alliance: Past, Present, and Future.* New York: Council on Foreign Relations.

Hoffman, David. 1999. "Clinton, Yeltsin Plan New Talks on Nuclear Arms." *Washington Post* (15 September): 2.

"A List of Japanese Companies Related to 'North Korean Arms.'" 1999. *Bungei Shunju* (August): 94–107. Available in English through the Foreign Broadcast Information Service, Document No. OW2207135399.

Manning, Robert A., and James J. Przystup. 1999. "Asia's Transition Diplomacy: Hedging Against Futureshock." *Survival* 41(3): 43–67.

Mazarr, Michael J. 1995. *North Korea and the Bomb: A Case Study in Nonproliferation.* New York: St. Martin's Press.

Oberdorfer, Don. 1997. *The Two Koreas: A Contemporary History.* Reading, Mass.: Addison-Wesley Publishers.

Sanger, David E. 1998. "North Korea Site an A-Bomb Plant, U.S. Agencies Say." *New York Times* (17 August): 1.

"Seoul Muses on Six-Nation Security Meeting." 1999. Xinhua. 7 October. Online. Lexis-Nexis. (7 October).

Sigal, Lee. 1998. *Disarming Strangers: Nuclear Diplomacy with North Korea.* Princeton, N.J.: Princeton University Press.

Snyder, Scott. 1996. "A Coming Crisis on the Korean Peninsula? The Food Crisis, Economic Decline, and Political Considerations." Special Report of the United States Institute of Peace.

———. 1999. "The Korean Peninsula Energy Development Organization: Implications for Northeast Asian Regional Security Cooperation?" Unpublished manuscript.

VI ♣ Violence and Major Power Coordination in Asia

Evan A. Feigenbaum

TEN YEARS AFTER THE COLLAPSE OF the Soviet Union, the central feature of international security remains the disjuncture between a peaceful Europe and an uncertain Asia. In Europe, the Balkan wars perennially threaten to flare into renewed fighting, yet the Balkans remain peripheral to European security, and fighting on the Balkan peninsula is mostly localized. In fact, 350 years after the Peace of Westphalia and the rise of the contemporary nation-state, the central security problems of Europe's major states west of the eastern Polish border have been solved (see Blackwill 1999; 2000, 109). Europe's major powers no longer menace each other; border disputes have disappeared amid European integration; joint armies, such as the Franco-German brigade, train for joint missions in the context of the North Atlantic Treaty Organization (NATO); and old national identities are increasingly in flux.

Asia, on the other hand, is far from such a peaceful regional status quo. The contrast between Europe and Asia in this sense is deeply rooted and runs in two separate dimensions. First, Asia's present situation mirrors some of the more destabilizing features of Europe's past. The key characteristics in Asia include:

- The shifting relative power balances among major states
- Uncertain alliance relationships
- A strategic environment driven by uncertainty instead of concrete threats
- Defense policies that hedge against uncertainty.

As Michael J. Green points out in his chapter on the revised Guidelines for U.S.-Japan Defense Cooperation, there is a strong tendency to focus on national defense at the expense of comprehensive security.

Second, strategic analysts invariably posit a potentially violent future for Asia. The elements that have historically fed Great Power strategic conflict—the most important of which are noted above—are now in place (e.g., see Freidberg 1993/1994). Most important, however, Asia lacks the deeply rooted security institutions of contemporary Europe, which anchor explanations of Europe's peaceful present and provide the underlying basis for doubts about future Asian stability (e.g., see Dibb, Hale, and Prince 1999).

In this chapter, I argue that strategic analysts of Asia ought to focus on the high likelihood of violence throughout Asia. But I also argue that these types of analyses have only half the story right; they know that Asia is unstable but obscure some of the most important reasons for this instability. Asia's future will likely be tremendously violent; in fact, Asia is already a violent region. But large-scale interstate conflict is not the source of the most destabilizing violence and is not likely to be so in the future.

Instead, although the Defense Guidelines, North Korean missile launches, and changing Chinese military posture and force projection capabilities are important, this chapter draws attention to a different set of concerns by arguing that the most telling security scenario of the past two years may, instead, be East Timor. On one level, of course, this seems fantastic, particularly in light of the very dangerous Taiwan problem. More important, this is not to argue that East Timor or a future blowup in Aceh will directly affect any of Northeast Asia's major states; in this particular situation, the consequences of political collapse—violence, refugee flows, and humanitarian pressures—will probably not reach beyond northern Australia and the southernmost Association of Southeast Nations (ASEAN) states.

Outside the Taiwan situation, only two real contingencies for large-scale interstate conflict appear to exist in contemporary Asia—the possibility of conflict on the Korean peninsula and between India and Pakistan. Meanwhile, five other forms of large-scale violence, in addition to interstate conflict and the special category of the Taiwan problem, threaten the capacity of Asia's major states to keep order in their strategic neighborhood:

• State collapse
• Internal ethnic violence

- Internal political violence
- Internal religious violence
- Violent humanitarian emergencies.

In short, whereas both the Korean peninsula and South Asia offer contingencies for interstate war, they also offer far more likely contingencies that mirror some of the conditions that have led to violent disaster in East Timor. In particular, the Timor situation suggests that collapsing polities and failed states are likely to account for most of the violence in Asia's future. Thus, Indonesia, Pakistan, and North Korea stand as examples of states that could well collapse and bring in their wake enormously high levels of violence.

Yet, if this is true, then China, Japan, and the United States—the "big powers" of the region—have failed to prepare for, much less confront (unilaterally, bilaterally, or trilaterally), the strategic consequences of the fact that Asia is likely to become increasingly violent in the future. However, this failure is largely for reasons unconnected to the large-scale interstate conflict that drives their military posture. The realities of growing violence in Asia, and the fact that few such violent Asian contingencies are connected to interstate war, expose the difficulties in China-Japan-U.S. cooperation. There is little that these countries have done, or are in a position to do, to cooperate to make Asia less violent.

This chapter offers three main propositions on ways to lessen violence in Asia.

- *With the exception of the Taiwan problem, only the Korean peninsula and South Asia offer contingencies for major interstate conflict.* This is in stark contrast to the cold war situation, when virtually the entire Asian security environment and the foreign policies and strategic choices of most Northeast and South Asian states were based almost exclusively on contingencies involving large-scale interstate war. Meanwhile, although the Southeast Asian states paid much greater attention to domestic security because of problems related to insurgency, these, too, often became entangled with the international politics of the cold war. We are now learning that this was true with China's critical involvement in Vietnam.[1]
- *As the prospects for interstate war fade, there are at least five potential categories for possible large-scale violence in Asia.*

• *There is little that China, Japan, or the United States has done to make Asia less violent or to prepare for any possibility of large-scale political and strategic instability in Asia that the major powers do not instigate.* This point, above all, should caution about the limits of trilateral cooperation. But, at the same time, it should also be a major focus of those who seek avenues for joint action. Thus, the final section of this chapter offers initial recommendations for bilateral and/or trilateral cooperation in these areas.

THE WANING OF
INTERSTATE CONTINGENCIES

To assert that Asian interstate conflict is on the wane does not in itself suggest that relations among the major Asia Pacific powers are likely to improve. Indeed, the reverse seems true, and strategic analysts should be under no illusions that relations between China, Japan, the Koreas (the Korean summit of June 2000 notwithstanding), and the United States are likely to be smooth in the coming years. China-U.S. relations, in particular, are in for a rocky ride, and not simply because the United States has a new administration that has made China policy part of its critique of its predecessor.[2] Rather, there is a growing recognition in Washington (and perhaps even in Beijing) that the problems at the core of the China-U.S. conflict have few, if any, short-term solutions and could be exacerbated by events beyond the control of policymakers in each capital.

In particular, pressure in Washington to move forward on national missile defense (NMD) and layered multiple-system theater missile defense (TMD) will continue to build in the years ahead, for the reasons that Scott Snyder details in his chapter on Korea's role in Northeast Asia. This development has little to do with existing technical reality per se; indeed, the technical record on missile defense remains highly mixed.

But the quest for effective NMD, in particular, drives the debate. Few serious analysts believe in the technical feasibility, or even strategic desirability, of a Ronald Reagan–style strategic defense initiative. However, because even the Clinton administration committed to discuss Anti-Ballistic Missile (ABM) Treaty revisions with Russia, the game is probably up for opponents of all forms of TMD and NMD, especially with the solid commitment of the Bush administration to pursue a range of missile defense options.

This is particularly true because President George W. Bush (1999) has declared publicly that he will unilaterally scrap U.S. commitment to the ABM Treaty if Russia does not agree to jointly approved revisions. No matter which party is in power in the United States—and no matter the technical and strategic merits or demerits of the missile defense concept—TMD and NMD almost certainly will proceed in some form and at some level of cost to the U.S. taxpayer. And because China has become an increasingly strident voice of opposition in the debate, arguments about this issue in the United States have, for a long time, ignored the concerns of those on the U.S. side who are most closely involved in China-U.S. relations. China policymakers have not driven the TMD and NMD debates; they have been forced to react to them.

Because TMD and NMD are likely to move forward, missile defense–related rhetoric will almost certainly be ratcheted up in the China-U.S. relationship. This will have important substantive consequences. Advocates of NMD are interested mainly in small numbers of interceptors; they recognize that missile defense can, in theory, be overwhelmed by both quantitative and qualitative adjustments in the Chinese arsenal. In the abstract, this ought to be stabilizing. However, the Chinese reaction has turned heavily on strategic intentions in addition to the potential for vulnerability. Increasingly, for example, defense policymakers in Beijing take as an article of faith that U.S. commitment to TMD signals something important about long-range intentions. This suspicion extends to TMD cooperation with Japan, and it will be particularly intense if discussion of some form of limited defense for Taiwan materializes. It is this sense of long-range strategic vulnerability, not the more limited capabilities of most TMD and NMD systems, that will inevitably lead China to seek both quantitative and qualitative improvements in its strategic arsenal—in addition to those that have been part of its regular force modernization program for the past fifteen years—no matter how the United States ultimately seeks to justify forward movement on various forms of missile defense. In turn, Chinese investments will escalate the rhetoric in the United States regarding China's emerging nuclear profile. Two important points to keep in mind are:

- There is growing pressure in the United States to offer Taiwan a more explicit defense commitment. Such a commitment may be conditional, but the mere existence of the debate will increase tension in the China-U.S. relationship.
- A variety of outstanding political and economic disputes will probably not be solved in the year ahead, China's World Trade Organization (WTO) entry notwithstanding.

Although strategic analysts must recognize that major power relations in Northeast Asia are tense for a number of reasons, the prospect of escalation to conflict has grown (and will continue to grow) increasingly likely.

The first reason for this increase in the likelihood of conflict involves the mixed dynamics of major power interaction. For all of their lack of strategic clarity, China, Japan, and the United States increasingly mix elements of rivalry with cooperation in their bilateral and trilateral interactions. It is reckless to assert that the problems of the post–cold war order—for example, economic geopolitics, globalization, and environmental challenges—vitiate the realities of major power competition. But they have made international relations increasingly complex. Thus, pure conflict models along cold war lines have limited value in thinking about the future of East Asia, in large part because mixed cooperation and rivalry are the realities of most state-to-state interaction (Feigenbaum 1999a).

To see this at work, one need only consider the evolution of Chinese technology policy in the past twenty years, which is tied in critical ways to the Chinese military's modernization agenda. The Chinese government has always been willing to purchase from abroad or to co-produce technologies with foreigners. This was true during the Mao Zedong years, and it remains true today. However, as a longer-range goal, freedom from external dependence has been the consistent and unwavering aim of the Chinese government. This "technonational" impulse flies in the face of China's growing integration into the global economy. And it also contains built-in contradictions because China must further integrate into international manufacturing, finance, and commerce to gain access to many of the technologies it seeks to indigenize (Feigenbaum 1999b).

Yet several structural impediments exist that will almost certainly restrain major interstate tension from escalating into out-and-out conflict.

The first of these impediments is the likelihood of a long-term U.S. forward presence. In the early 1990s, the U.S. commitment to Asia Pacific seemed increasingly fragile, especially militarily as the closure of its Philippine bases and debates about burden-sharing hinted at the possibility of a scaled-back U.S. commitment. Yet as Robert Blackwill (2000, 117) has argued, presently there is no significant political pressure in the United States to reduce the American strategic commitment to Asia. In particular, the waning of "consequential threats" to vital American interests in Europe has led to a shift in U.S. strategic attention to Asia and the Middle East.

In effect, this analysis suggests a much longer-term U.S. military involvement in the region than seemed likely just five years ago. And it is largely independent of the precise number of U.S. forces— 100,000 seems an increasingly arbitrary number, not only because of the revolution in military affairs (RMA) but also because of substantial U.S. capabilities in lift and other forms of power projection (on the impact of the RMA in Asia, see Dibb 1997/1998).

The realities of the U.S. presence suggest a critical constraint on interstate war. Pressure to prevent the rise of another hegemonic power will most likely keep U.S. forces actively deployed in the region. Concerns about weapons of mass destruction (WMD) proliferation further promote missile defense efforts. Yet the U.S. presence remains a stabilizing feature of the Asian security environment. This is ironic for a number of reasons—most notably, for reasons of concrete strategic and economic interests, a strong counterproliferation commitment, implicit commitments to Taiwan's defense, and concern in certain quarters of the U.S. administration and Congress about emerging Chinese power. These reasons also happen to be the precise features of American policy that China most deeply resents. This approach bodes ill for China-U.S. relations, yet it has few implications for regional instability, and almost certainly acts as a stabilizing feature. The U.S. commitment discourages the expansion of Japanese military power, guarantees open Asian sea lines of communication, offers a blanket to those countries concerned about the accommodation of China within the regional security system, and provides at least an implicit commitment to Taiwan.

INWARD PREOCCUPATION

A second major constraint on interstate war in Asia is the preoccupation of regional leaders with internal problems. The Asian financial crisis of 1997–1999 exacerbated this trend. Restored growth notwithstanding, the underlying causes of Chinese, Japanese, South Korean, and Southeast Asian economic and political uncertainty remain in place. Even as some growth has returned, the political will to take painful adjustments has dissipated in many countries of the region.[3] Thus, although some countries have the potential to capitalize on technological developments elsewhere, and there are signs of further deregulation and market opening, guaranteed high economic growth rates in Asia are a thing of the past.

Chinese leaders must confront the fundamental problems of structural reform in an atmosphere of slowed growth and shrinking domestic demand. In Japan, the economic recession is continuing, but the politicians still have failed to attack structural weaknesses in the financial system. Most Southeast Asian countries are internally focused, but still have not confronted the domestic aspects of economic uncertainty, and therefore remain vulnerable to volatility in international capital markets.

LACK OF IRREDENTISM
OVER CORE TERRITORIAL CLAIMS

Third, past territorial claims are a major source of potential tension. However, the Taiwan conflict does not involve the territorial claims of another power. The U.S. commitment to Taiwan is founded on other issues. There are, in fact, extant territorial disputes between major powers of the region, including China and India, Japan and Russia, and even Japan and the Koreas. But with the sole exception of

India and Pakistan, none of the major powers in Asia insists on claims to core territories of any major strategic significance. Russo-Japanese disputes focus on the Northern Territories (as the Japanese refer to them), which have symbolic and historical significance but are strategically and economically inconsequential. The China-India dispute concerns large parcels of territory on both sides of their disputed border, but in an isolated Himalayan mountain region, and the overall strategic significance of such isolated territory has probably declined in the face of the emerging Sino-Indian nuclear competition. The China-Japan dispute over the Senkaku Islands (or Diaoyutai, in Chinese) also focuses on a largely peripheral set of territorial claims. This is also true of the Spratlys, of major Southeast Asian claims, and even of claims in Central Asia, such as the China-Kazakhstan border disputes, which were essentially solved in 1998.

STABLE DETERRENCE

Finally, the central feature of the Asian strategic environment remains overwhelming U.S. military superiority. With the TMD and NMD debates likely to accelerate in the United States, Chinese force projection investments will also undoubtedly increase.

Yet at least some of the central features of strategic deterrence are already in place in East Asia. China is under no substantive threat of direct attack, and charges of strategic vulnerability to TMD are less convincing than are Chinese concerns about what the U.S. commitment to TMD signals about its intentions. The tactical reality is that only the most expensive versions of TMD and NMD from among those currently under discussion could not be overwhelmed by a combination of significant quantitative and qualitative improvements to existing Chinese strategic forces. By design, current plans for upper-tier defenses are focused primarily on defeating small numbers of missiles. This would not be comforting to China. But it does suggest that Chinese concerns about TMD, while important, do not reflect short-term strategic vulnerability. NMD is a more complex matter. But the American presence, coupled with overwhelming U.S. military superiority, provides some element of comfort to those who worry about the integration of China into the regional order.

SOURCES OF ASIAN INSTABILITY AND VIOLENCE

In light of these constraints, it is important to question whether the sources of strategic collapse in Asia over the next five to seven years are likely to come from traditional forms of interstate competition. Indeed, the focus on interstate contingencies has obscured the reality of other forms of large-scale violence in Asia with strategic consequences that will resonate throughout the region.

For purposes of discussion, these can be divided into four main categories that capture most forms of political violence in Asia today: interstate war; the Taiwan contingency (which is not an interstate problem but if it escalates to military conflict, will almost certainly come to involve other states); state collapse; and internal ethnic, political, religious, or humanitarian emergency–related violence.

It is difficult to imagine any contingencies in the category of interstate war, at least under present circumstances, aside from war on the Korean peninsula and the more real prospect of Indo-Pakistani conflict in South Asia. Yet both of these contingencies present opportunities for trilateral coordination and will likely remain localized for the time being. A Korean contingency would almost certainly firm up coordination between Japan and the United States. China—always uncomfortable with U.S. military action, and no doubt especially squeamish about action so close to home—has long since accepted the reality of an American response to major cross-border provocation from North Korea. However, no new major power Korean war is in the cards, and the historic June 2000 summit between the North and South has given new reason for hope for an eventual peaceful reunification process. In addition, the North Korean nuclear problem has provided several new avenues for strategic coordination that have built a measure of stability into trilateral interactions on the peninsula.

South Asia is no less difficult strategically, but it crosscuts what are essentially shared vital interests for all other Asian states. For China, Japan, and the United States, in particular, the core issues in South Asia concern WMD, not the Indo-Pakistani conflict per se. Thus, the prospect of a war in South Asia threatens to undermine the taboo against nuclear use, could lead to the collapse of Pakistan, and thereby poses a shared policy challenge to the major powers of the region.

The Taiwan issue is beyond the scope of this chapter but is detailed in Gregory C. May's chapter on the Taiwan factor in trilateral big power relations. So long as it is not militarized, however, Taiwan need not be viewed as a primarily interstate problem. Under present circumstances, though, it is virtually impossible to envision a major military contingency involving a large-scale use of force against Taiwan in which U.S. forces would not become involved. For Chinese and Americans, this is an unfortunate possibility. Taiwan is indeed a matter to be settled peacefully among Chinese on both sides of the Taiwan Strait, but this assessment obscures the reality of U.S. involvement in the Taiwan problem. Taiwan may be China's internal affair, but the United States has been involved in the situation since 1949, and has legal, political, historical, and moral commitments there. Despite considerable hand-wringing about whether the new Guidelines for U.S.-Japan Defense Cooperation might extend Japanese logistical support to the United States in a Taiwan contingency, it is difficult to conceive how it could be otherwise. Thomas Christensen (1999) has noted that Washington may, in such a contingency, wish to leave Japan out of the affair. Japanese participation could be the tinderbox that causes more political and strategic problems than the logistical challenges it would help to solve.

Still, the dynamics that would shape Japan's ultimate role in such a contingency may lie, largely, with decision makers in Washington. It is difficult to conceive how Japan could refuse to provide any support to U.S. forces in a Taiwan contingency if requested to do so. Japan's participation might be limited, symbolic, and largely token in military value, but Japan is the major American alliance partner in East Asia. To refuse to support the United States in what is probably the most important potential contingency for U.S. forces in the region would probably destroy the roots of the Japan-U.S. alliance.

Because Taiwan is among the most likely sources of interstate conflict in East Asia, then, it is more imperative than ever to see that a peaceful status quo continues. However, the political and military choices that this requires for China, Japan, the United States, and Taiwan are beyond the scope of this essay (for information on some of the issues prior to China's 1995–1996 missile exercise, see Feigenbaum 1995). Instead, in a strategic environment in which traditional interstate forms of violence seem increasingly unlikely, it is the Timor situation and possible analogues throughout the region that suggest the most likely causes of large-scale strategic collapse in Asia. Most other violent contingencies revolve around the issues of collapsing polities and failed states. The most likely scenarios of collapse involve Indonesia, Pakistan, and North Korea, but there are others for which collapse would bring violence in their wake as well and thus have major effects on the strategic environment in Asia.

From the economic-political dimension, Indonesia is a case in point, for in Indonesia such collapse would represent an almost total failure of the strategic glue (economic growth) that has formed the basis of cooperative interstate relations in Asia since 1945. Collapsing states would make clear that domestic growth alone cannot build secure polities. Past growth rates would be meaningless if subsequent growth stalls and popular welfare declines (this lesson should resonate in China, in particular).

The real prospect of large-scale internal violence and state failure also has a political dimension: It would demonstrate that politics can ultimately trump economics, whether for reasons of ethnic, religious, national, or political loyalty. This lesson speaks to several countries of the region, including Indonesia, Pakistan, China, the Philippines, Malaysia, India, Thailand, Myanmar, Bangladesh, Cambodia, and Laos.

Finally, these non-interstate sources of Asian violence threaten to overwhelm more stable states in a morass of humanitarian woes, ranging from refugee flows to piracy. In this vein, it is worth noting, as so many South Korean analysts often do, that a North Korean collapse could itself reshape the strategic environment of the region. Violent conflagration and collapse, not merely interstate conflict on the peninsula, pose strategic challenges that resonate regionwide.

Beyond state collapse, one category of four related issues—all of which foreshadow state collapse—are already responsible for large amounts of violence throughout Asia: internal ethnic, political, and religious violence, and humanitarian emergencies.

These are not restricted to peripheral areas or to countries where violence is comparatively simple to localize, such as Myanmar. At least three of these contingencies—ethnic, political, and religious violence —apply to China. Several could come to apply to North Korea in the next three to five years. And all categories currently apply to India, Indonesia, Pakistan, Bangladesh, and Myanmar.

The Lack of Trilateral Coordination —
Prescriptions for Change

In light of the consequences of political violence, it is extraordinary that, as various forms of violence have accelerated in Asia, China, Japan, and the United States find themselves in virtually no position to shape a regional environment that prevents these occurrences.

Indonesia offers the most poignant example, among many: in 1998, when the Suharto government fell amid an orgy of anti-Chinese violence; in 1999, when East Timor made clear just how poorly equipped the international system was to respond to state anarchy; and in Aceh. In Timor, of course, strategic commitments to Indonesia trumped humanitarian and political commitments. This was hardly surprising. But it bodes ill for future coordination as Aceh deteriorates, and it has also produced a major debate in the region about U.S. roles and commitments on these issues. The comments of one leading Australian politician are telling in this regard: "While the U.S. may be the strongest armed force in the world, it could not have been weaker in its initial response to Australia's request for assistance with East Timor during September 1999" (Fischer 2000). For the future, strategic commitments remain paramount for the trilateral countries.

If Timor is seen not merely as a humanitarian conflagration but as a strategic challenge that foreshadows state collapse and extraordinarily high levels of violence that could, in other countries and in other contingencies, spill over their borders, then the Timor experience takes on strategic dimensions that are relevant in a trilateral context.

Simply put, China, Japan, and the United States are ill-equipped to do anything about such violence. They have yet to put in place a substantive capacity to respond—unilaterally (witness the Chinese experience in 1998 in Indonesia and the U.S. response in Timor in 1999), bilaterally, or trilaterally. In addition, they remain unwilling (and unlikely) to seek ways to do so for the following reasons:

- China hews to a "hyper-sovereignty" (Johnston 1998, 2) stance that disdains the precedent of any interference in internal affairs.[4]
- Japan has virtually no levers of direct influence at its disposal and is especially preoccupied in the wake of its economic crisis. Most

important, it is restrained by normative commitments to non-interference that are different from China's concern with sovereignty but ultimately produce the same result—noninterference.

• The United States has routinely been ineffective in such situations. Unilateralism would raise Chinese hackles, whereas bilateralism and multilateralism have often been met with distrust (not just in China). Australian and U.S. action in Timor (which was tentative at best) produced a barrage of criticism from around Southeast Asia.

This inability to respond is unfortunate. These are contingencies that will likely grow in importance and, more significantly, account for virtually all of the violence that destabilizes individual Asian countries, and potentially the region, over the next several years. Even China is not immune to any of these trends.

But if such problems suggest at least some avenues for partnership and coordination, the trilateral countries have few, if any, levers of influence at their disposal. China, Japan, and the United States—individually, as well as together—have long since shown themselves ill-disposed to use what limited policy levers they have. This poses a serious challenge to advocates of trilateral coordination and also reflects a lack of political will. There are steps that could be taken to begin laying a foundation for greater cooperation with respect to these types of threats.

As a first step, and with due regard to Chinese concern about noninterference in the internal affairs of sovereign states, cooperative efforts should focus on two areas: counterterrorism and humanitarian relief.

COUNTERTERRORISM

China and the United States should, on a bilateral basis, expand and enhance the scope of their law enforcement cooperation in areas related to counterterrorism. However, because the United States must be careful not to enhance Chinese tactical capabilities that could be used in the suppression of domestic dissent, this should be done in a highly targeted fashion, and within two constraints: (1) coordination should be focused on common threats, concentrating on threats that both sides view as a potential terrorist challenge that requires enhanced information sharing for preemption and suppression, and

(2) joint cooperation should be focused primarily on informational, rather than tactical, aspects of law enforcement and policing.

The United States should open a Federal Bureau of Investigation (FBI) Legal Attaché Office in Beijing. Such an office already exists in Hong Kong, and a firm basis exists to build on previous China-U.S. law enforcement coordination.[5]

On a trilateral basis, China, Japan, and the United States should also enhance law enforcement coordination related to counterterrorism. Japan's Aum Shinrikyō experience proves that Japan faces many counterterrorism challenges that China and the United States also share.

The legacy of the Aum attack on the Tokyo subway also provides a basis to enhance coordination on countering WMD terrorism, more specifically. The trilateral countries should consider ways to enhance four-way coordination with Russia on these issues.

Especially in light of the shared China-U.S. concern about Islamic extremism, the trilateral countries should jointly seek to enhance their relationships with law enforcement agencies in Central and South Asia and the Middle East, in particular. China, Russia, Kazakhstan, Tajikistan, and the Kyrgyz Republic, for example, have already declared their intention to deepen counterterrorism coordination related to the Shanghai Five. China should seek more institutionalized ways to enhance its coordination in that forum with efforts by Japan and the United States on shared concerns (Feigenbaum 2001, 29).

HUMANITARIAN RELIEF

China, Japan, and the United States should begin a more institutionalized dialogue at the level of the assistant secretaries of state and defense on specific contingencies in which China might actively participate in humanitarian peacekeeping. Such dialogue should not shy away from the key points of policy division but should seek contingencies and standard response procedures in which they can be reconciled.

For Washington, these considerations focus on concerns about subordinating U.S. contributions to UN oversight. Thus, the United States should, as Blackwill (2000, 132) has urged, seriously consider as its working assumption the notion that all peacekeeping/peacemaking in Asia should be under the auspices of the UN Security Council.

For Japan, concerns in this area tie into recent peacekeeping operations (PKO) debates. However, Japan should make a decision to enhance its PKO contributions. The main concerns for the Chinese touch on sovereignty. But there are cases, specifically related to genocide, where Chinese analysts have indicated some flexibility. Enhanced three-way discussion of these issues should therefore begin by focusing on principled contingencies related to genocide. Discussion should then seek to expand the range of contingencies outward to embrace a broader number of contingencies in which the authority and/or legitimacy of a sovereign government breaks down in the context of a humanitarian emergency.

Institutionally, China, Japan, and the United States should seek, on a trilateral basis, to enhance their ability to coordinate deliveries of food and medical relief. The U.S. Federal Emergency Management Agency (FEMA) should deepen institutionalized dialogue and exchange on relief methods and tactics. There is much precedent here on which to build: China has extensive relief experience in North Korea and in its own prior efforts related to flood control and other natural disasters. Japan's experience with the Tokaimura nuclear accident and other past contingencies reflects a range of experience. Similarly, the United States has extensive experience in the area of humanitarian relief.

These prescriptions represent initial, sometimes partial, steps in just two areas of concern. But although external sources of conflict may divide China, Japan, and the United States on the key geostrategic issues of the Asia Pacific region, it is the many internal sources of violence that seem most likely to cause political breakdown in the future. This poses a challenge to all three countries. But because these issues directly crosscut a number of trilaterally shared interests and concerns, they also provide an important platform for enhanced three-way coordination.

Notes

1. Domestic insurgencies, aided and abetted by external actors, figured large in the security concerns of, for example, Thailand, the Philippines, and Malaysia throughout the cold war. But as a painstaking and seminal new study of Sino-Vietnamese relations also makes clear, the momentum of Vietnamese moves, for example, was

decisively influenced by the dynamics of outside powers' commitments and concerns (see Qiang 2000).

2. The essence of this critique is that the notion of a China-U.S. strategic partnership is fantastical; in fact, China and the United States are long-term strategic competitors that do nonetheless share some interests where cooperation will be required.

3. Commentary from Peter Geithner has helped me to understand the potential sources of renewed growth in the future. But as he has noted, in personal communication, there are developments in the international arena that will affect the momentum for reform and force further changes in Asian economies even if their growth rates do increase again. In particular, Geithner notes, the increased reliance on equity finance and the need to intermediate huge sums of capital as countries shift from defined benefit to defined contribution pension schemes is revolutionizing capital markets with the attendant requirements of greater transparency and accountability.

4. There were some initial positive signs from the Timor experience that suggest this might be less intractable than some analysts have implied. But it is important to note the absolutely critical distinction that Chinese analysts make in justifying Chinese support for the Timor operation. In numerous personal communications with Chinese diplomats and analysts, in China and the United States, the following theme has recurred: A sovereign state, Indonesia, itself invited the UN force into Timor. Thus, UN operations did not violate, from the Chinese standpoint, what are mostly nonnegotiable principles of sovereignty and noninterference.

5. There is a solid record of prior coordination between the FBI, local U.S. police, the Hong Kong police, and China's Ministry of Public Security. The most prominent example is the effort to suppress the organized crime activities of the New York–based Green Dragons. In the early 1990s, after the United States obtained Racketeer Influenced and Corrupt Organization Act (RICO) indictments against the leader and thirteen other members of the group on charges including seven murders, two home robberies, extortion, kidnapping, bribery, conspiracy, and illegal gambling, China arrested the leader and moved to prosecute him in China under tough Chinese anti–organized crime laws. There is also an extensive prior record of China-U.S. coordination on immigration fraud. In one important case, the FBI and the Immigration and Naturalization Service (INS) deported to China for trial the leader of a massive fraud racket and repatriated to China millions of dollars stolen in the scheme (see Freeh 1995). On broad issues in China-U.S. law enforcement cooperation, see, for example, Yeung (undated).

BIBLIOGRAPHY

Blackwill, Robert D. 1999. *The Future of Transatlantic Relations.* New York: Council on Foreign Relations.

———. 2000. "An Action Agenda to Strengthen America's Alliances in the Asia Pacific Region." In Robert D. Blackwill and Paul Dibb, eds. *America's Asian Alliances.* Cambridge, Mass.: MIT Press.

Bush, George W. 1999. Speech at The Citadel. 25 September.

Christensen, Thomas J. 1999. "China, the U.S.-Japan Alliance, and the Security Dilemma in East Asia." *International Security* 23(4): 49–80.

Dibb, Paul. 1997/1998. "The Revolution in Military Affairs and Asia's Security." *Survival* 39(4): 93–116.

Dibb, Paul, David D. Hale, and Peter Prince. 1999. "Asia's Insecurity." *Survival* 41(3): 5–20.

Feigenbaum, Evan A. 1995. *Change in Taiwan and Potential Adversity in the Strait.* Santa Monica, Calif.: RAND.

———. 1999a. "China's Military Posture and the New Economic Geopolitics." *Survival* 41(2): 71–88.

———. 1999b. "Who's Behind China's High-Technology 'Revolution'? How Bomb Makers Remade Beijing's Priorities, Policies, and Institutions." *International Security* 24(1): 95–126.

———. 2001. "China's Strategy of Weakness." *Far Eastern Economic Review.* (1 March).

Fischer, Tim. 2000. "Mighty Washington's Show of Weakness." *Australian Financial Review* (1 February).

Freeh, Louis J. 1995. Speech to the 17th Annual International Asian Organized Crime Conference. Boston, Mass. 6 March. <http://www.fbi.gov/pressrm/dirspch95/asian.htm> (1 February 2000).

Freidberg, Aaron. 1993/1994. "Ripe for Rivalry: Prospects for Peace in a Multipolar Asia." *International Security* 18(3): 5–33.

Johnston, Alastair Iain. 1998. "China's Militarized Interstate Dispute Behavior, 1949–1992: A First Cut at the Data." *China Quarterly* (153): 1–30.

Qiang Zhai. 2000. *China and the Vietnam Wars, 1950–1975.* Chapel Hill, N.C.: University of North Carolina Press.

Yeung, W. Undated. "What Method of Communication Will Be Used to Combat Chinese Organized Crime Enterprises between Law Enforcement Agencies in California and China by 2005?" California Law Enforcement Command College Independent Studies, no. 21–0443.

About the Contributors

DAVID M. LAMPTON is George and Sadie Hyman Professor and Director of China Studies at Johns Hopkins University's Paul H. Nitze School of Advanced International Studies (SAIS), and Director of the China Studies Program at The Nixon Center. Dr. Lampton is also a member of the Council on Foreign Relations, and serves on the Board of Directors of the National Committee on U.S.-China Relations. Previously, Dr. Lampton was President of the National Committee on U.S.-China Relations, Inc. (1988–1997), Director of the China Policy Program, American Enterprise Institute (1985–1987), and Associate Professor at Ohio State University (1979–1987). Dr. Lampton is a graduate of Stanford University, where he received his B.A., M.A., and Ph.D.; he also received an Honorary Doctorate from the Institute of Far East Studies, Russian Academy of Sciences. His numerous publications include *Same Bed, Different Dreams: Managing U.S.-China Relations, 1989-2000* (2001) and *The Making of Chinese Foreign and Security Policy in the Era of Reform: 1978-2000* (ed., 2001).

AMY P. CELICO is a political officer stationed in Shanghai for the U.S. Department of State. Previously she was analyst of North Korean affairs at the U.S. Department of State Bureau of Intelligence and Research. Ms. Celico earned an M.A. in Strategic Studies and International Economics from Johns Hopkins University's Paul H. Nitze School of Advanced International Studies (SAIS), where she focused on East Asian security issues.

EVAN A. FEIGENBAUM is Executive Director of the Asia-Pacific Security Initiative at Harvard University's John F. Kennedy School of

Government. He also serves as Program Chair of the School's Chinese Security Studies Program. He has taught Chinese foreign policy and comparative nuclear weapons policy at Harvard as Lecturer on Government in the Faculty of Arts and Sciences. He also taught on the Faculty of National Security Affairs of the U.S. Naval Postgraduate School, and was Executive Secretary of the non-partisan Australian-American Leadership Dialogue Task Force on the future of the alliance. His most recent publications include *China's Techno-Warriors: National Security and Strategic Competition from the Nuclear to the Information Age* (forthcoming) and *Change in Taiwan and Potential Adversity in the Strait* (1995). Dr. Feigenbaum received his Ph.D. in Political Science from Stanford University. He was a 1997–1998 John M. Olin Fellow in National Security at Harvard, and a 1994–1997 fellow at Stanford's Center for International Security and Arms Control. He is a term member of the Council on Foreign Relations, a member of the National Committee on U.S.-China Relations, and a member of the U.S. committee of the Council for Security Cooperation in the Asia-Pacific.

MICHAEL J. GREEN completed his chapter while Senior Fellow for Asian Security Studies at the Council on Foreign Relations and lecturer in East Asian Studies at the Paul H. Nitze School of Advanced International Studies (SAIS) of Johns Hopkins University. He has since joined the National Security Council as Director for Asian Affairs (the views expressed in the book are his own). Dr. Green received his M.A. from SAIS in 1987 and his Ph.D. in 1994. Dr. Green's most recent books and monographs include *State of the Field Report: Research on Japanese Security Policy* (1998); *The U.S.-Japan Alliance: Past, Present, and Future* (co-edited, 1999); and *Reluctant Realism: Japan's Foreign Policy in an Era of Uncertain Power* (2001).

GREGORY C. MAY is a former Assistant Director and Research Associate in Chinese Studies at The Nixon Center. In September 2000, Mr. May joined the United States Foreign Service and is currently serving at the United States Consulate General in Guangzhou, China. The views expressed in this book are his alone and do not represent the official position of the United States government. Mr. May received his M.A. in China Studies from Johns Hopkins

University's Paul H. Nitze School of Advanced International Studies in 1998 and his B.A. in Chinese from the University of Texas at Austin in 1992.

DANIEL H. ROSEN is a Visiting Fellow at the Institute for International Economics (IIE) in Washington, D.C., where he focuses on China and on the New Economy. Previously he was Senior Advisor for International Economic Policy at the White House National Economic Council (NEC). Prior to joining the NEC, he was Director of Research and Corporate Development at *ChinaOnline*, where he helped build the firm's information products. He was a Research Fellow at IIE until 1999, when his book *Behind the Open Door: Foreign Enterprises in the Chinese Marketplace* was co-published by IIE and the Council on Foreign Relations. He writes and speaks extensively on U.S.-China economic relations. He has worked at IBM Governmental Relations, the U.S. International Trade Administration, and the Woodrow Wilson Center for Scholars. He is a member of the Council on Foreign Relations and the National Committee for U.S.-China Relations.

SCOTT SNYDER is Representative to the Korea Office of the Asia Foundation in Seoul, Korea. He is an active writer and commentator on Asian security issues with a special focus on Korea. Previously, Mr. Snyder was an Asia specialist in the Research and Studies Program of the U.S. Institute of Peace (USIP), and was a recipient of the Abe Fellowship, a research program administered by the Social Sciences Research Council. His book entitled *Negotiating on the Edge: North Korean Negotiating Behavior* was published by USIP Press in 1999. Prior to his work at USIP, Mr. Snyder was Acting Director of the Contemporary Affairs Department of the Asia Society. He received his B.A. from Rice University and an M.A. from the Regional Studies East Asia Program at Harvard University. He was the recipient of a Thomas G. Watson Fellowship in 1987–1988 and attended Yonsei University in South Korea.

Index

Anti-Ballistic Missile (ABM) Treaty, 16, 108, 116–117
ASEAN Regional Forum (ARF), 9, 33–34, 41
Asian financial crisis (1997–1999), 88, 104, 120
Asian instability, 113, 122
Asia-Pacific Economic Cooperation (APEC) forum, 9, 34, 56–57, 78–79, 101, 105
Association of Southeast Asian Nations (ASEAN), 34, 114

Bush, George, 28–29, 55, 75–76
Bush, George W., 103, 117

Chen Shui-bian, 11, 17, 47, 50, 63, 65, 91
China
  defense strategy, 25, 59; and Asian financial crisis, 88, 90, 96; security strategy: national, 31, regional, 34; view of Asian financial crisis, 28; view of Japan-U.S. ties, 60, 73, 79, 83; view of U.S.: leadership, 30, 32, NATO actions, 26, 36
China-Japan relations, 15, 58, 62, 69n. 8, 104–105, 108, 110
  and reaction to revision of U.S.-Japan Defense Guidelines, 39, 82; and South Korea, 110, 116; in wake of Asian financial crisis, 89
China-Japan-U.S. relations, 19, 87–88, 109, 115, 118
  and Asian financial crisis, 90, 95; economic, 91, 93–94, 96; and humanitarian peacekeeping, 127; and Islamic extremism, 127; and Korean peninsula, 92, 97; lack of coordination, 88, 115, 125, 127; and law enforcement, 126–127; and response

to violence, 125; and Taiwan, 12–14, 45, 62, 67, 91
China-South Korea relations, 105
China-Taiwan relations
  economic ties, 53, 92; interaction mechanisms, 63, 65–66; tensions, 45, 53, 58, 67
China-U.S. relations, 59, 62, 109, 116, 119
  bombing of Chinese embassy, 24, 36; counterterrorism, 126; ideological differences, 24, 26, 28, 38–39; normalization of relations (1979), 54; and North Korea, 100; shared tenets, 25, 27–28, 37–38; tensions: 116–117, over Kosovo, 23, 35, over Taiwan, 61; in wake of Asian financial crisis, 89
Clinton, Bill, 11, 27, 29–30, 50, 55–56, 61, 76, 78–79, 81, 90, 101, 103, 111n. 1, 116

Deng Xiaoping, 30–31, 53

East Timor, 10, 38, 114–115, 125

Guidelines for U.S.-Japan Defense Cooperation, 24, 39, 74, 79, 113, 123
  revision of, 74, 78–79, 81, 83–84

Hashimoto Ryūtarō, 69n. 6, 78
Hata Tsutomu, 77
Hosokawa Morihiro, 69n. 6, 76

Indonesia, 124–125
international security environment, 27

Japan
  approach to security, 76, 80, 84, 108; and Asian financial crisis, 89, 96; National

Japan Center for
International Exchange

FOUNDED IN 1970, the Japan Center for International Exchange (JCIE) is an independent, nonprofit, and nonpartisan organization dedicated to strengthening Japan's role in international affairs. JCIE believes that Japan faces a major challenge in augmenting its positive contributions to the international community, in keeping with its position as one of the world's largest industrial democracies. Operating in a country where policymaking has traditionally been dominated by the government bureaucracy, JCIE has played an important role in broadening debate on Japan's international responsibilities by conducting international and cross-sectional programs of exchange, research, and discussion.

JCIE creates opportunities for informed policy discussions; it does not take policy positions. JCIE programs are carried out with the collaboration and cosponsorship of many organizations. The contacts developed through these working relationships are crucial to JCIE's efforts to increase the number of Japanese from the private sector engaged in meaningful policy research and dialogue with overseas counterparts. JCIE receives no government subsidies; rather, funding comes from private foundation grants, corporate contributions, and contracts.